The DbD Experience

First, pick up a copy of Rachel Rosenthal's inspiring *The DbD Experience*—part manual, part manifesto, part memoir—then head for Los Angeles . . .

Friday: Origins

Arrive at the "Doing by Doing" workshop to be greeted by Rosenthal—pioneering theater explorer and your host for the weekend ahead. Explore non-human ways of living and moving. Begin to develop a shared vocabulary with your fellow students through exercises.

Saturday: Connections

Continue to connect with the group on an energetic level. Make the journey from Kansas to Oz. Collaborate and create as a group—moving and vocalizing without language. Improvise boldly at every step. Treat music, voice, lighting, costume, sets, props and fellow performers as equals.

Sunday: Power

Learn to arrive in the moment when you are needed. Engage with transformative processes and take part in the Star Meditation. Understand your own individual power, joining your physical and emotional self. Perform solo improvisations and the Rambler—the final, extended culmination of everything that you have learned through the 34 hour experience.

The DbD Experience

Chance knows what it's doing!

Rachel Rosenthal

Edited and with a foreword by Kate Noonan

Routledge
Taylor & Francis Group
LONDON AND NEW YORK

First published 2010 by Routledge

2 Park Square, Milton Park, Abingdon, Oxfordshire OX14 4RN
52 Vanderbilt Avenue, New York, NY 10017

Routledge is an imprint of the Taylor & Francis Group, an informa business

First issued in paperback 2018

Typeset in GillSans by
Keystroke, Tettenhall, Wolverhampton

British Library Cataloguing in Publication Data
A catalogue record for this book is available from the British Library

Library of Congress Cataloging in Publication Data
Rosenthal, Rachel, 1926–
The DbD experience book : chance knows what it's doing! /
Rachel Rosenthal; edited with foreword by Kate Noonan.
p. cm.
1. Improvisation (Acting) I. Title.
PN2071.I5R67 2009
792.02'8—dc22 2009006997

ISBN13: 978-0-415-55101-4 (hbk)
ISBN13: 978-0-415-55102-1 (pbk)

To Dibidi with all my love

Contents

Foreword

Kate Noonan

> Moments come when we feel outside time, seized by a longing, moved by an image, in touch with invisible voices. We realize that we do not live in one world only. As Rilke says, "we are grasped by what we cannot grasp . . ." Something beyond life lives within life and calls the soul.
>
> James Hillman

Rachel Rosenthal in *Traps*, 1982. Photo by Daniel Joseph Martinez

I first encountered Rachel Rosenthal in the late 1980s in an ad for her DbD (Doing by Doing) workshop in the *LA Weekly*: a bald woman in fatigues, her cavernous mouth contorted in a scream—that image scared the hell out of me. The ferocity and raw power of that photograph, along with the text promising an *intensive* experience made me so very uncomfortable that I had to question *why* it made me so uncomfortable (I was reading James Hillman at the time).

That ad became a sort of emblem for my fears, confessed to a friend who laughed with me about how uneasy it made me feel, and at me and my pronouncement that since it frightened me so much, that was reason enough for me to sign up and confront it (James Hillman's idea).

I didn't rush to sign up, however. Confronting my fear was theoretical at that point.

My theater background was firmly rooted in realism. I was taught that one started from theme—the Big Idea. An actor's mandate was to serve the playwright. The action took place in rooms with a fourth wall. The sets were tables and chairs. I had studied in New York with Stella Adler and was steeped in Ibsen, Strindberg and Shaw. My personal tastes ran more toward Beckett, Peter Handke and Ionesco, yet I was a devoted student of Stella's acting maxim; "Understanding leads to doing, doing leads to experience" (as in experiencing the emotion, the truth of the circumstance). I was then, and remain, a devotee of the written word. Content was everything. Form (or as we would say the "How") would follow as a result (and was largely in my opinion the director's problem).

As is the truth in many an actor's circumstance, I sometimes made my living teaching. I worked with adult actors and with children in various programs and settings, from scene study and technique in conservatory to summer theater camp. It was after one intense and exhausting summer camp session for inner city youth that I decided to confront the fear and sign up for the DbD Experience, as its dates happened to fall on the weekend I would be heading home. Camp ended Friday morning, I would drive straight to the DbD. The children in that particular session inspired me by their willingness to commit themselves wholeheartedly to something utterly foreign to their experience.

Unbeknownst to me, a friend of mine had also signed on for the DbD weekend. We had had similar training—he had been a student of Sanford Meisner's in New York. I was happily surprised to see him at the studio when I arrived, and I latched on to him like a vise.

Rachel, too, was a surprise. Here was no boot camp warrior general, but a rather lovely middle-aged woman with a vaguely European accent, dressed with panache, bedecked in jewelry, and trailed by two large friendly dogs. I remember she was gracious and welcoming. I remember little else about that first evening, only that I felt very much a stranger in a strange land.

The exercises were non-verbal, and—uh-oh—touchy-feely.

I was *extremely* uncomfortable.

Shy and admittedly somewhat bookish by nature, I had always been a good student—a quick study. Here, I was worse than remedial—I simply did not get it and it was exasperating. Rachel gave feedback to the students who all seemed to understand what she was after and what was meant. I struggled to identify an urgency that propelled the processes and found none. Had my friend not been there I am certain I would not have returned the following morning and would have dismissed the work as nonsense. He, like the other students, was enthusiastic and excited, which fueled my suspicion that the deficit was mine. I did some psychological reshuffling, shifted my identity gears from expert to tourist and attempted to "go with the flow".

Saturday was better. I began to notice that when Rachel gave feedback she talked about form: composition, tension, shape. She asked us to be aware of our partnerships on an energetic rather than a psychological level. The work was more kin to the visual arts than to the theater I had heretofore been working in.

Rachel insisted that the lights, the set, the audience, the music, gravity and air—elements I had never given much thought to—were all in this together, and there was no hierarchy, no one element more important than the next. As the weekend progressed, I experienced moments of hope and despair, clarity and confusion, chaos and beauty. And play for its own sake, which was a revelation.

What was being offered in the workshop was the abstract underpinnings of Theater. A different kind of scaffolding, metaphorical and poetic, imagistic, surreal.

Realism lost its luster. I went from Kansas to Oz and never looked back.

Stella had been after a theatrical truth, trying (and with her fellow members of the Group Theater, succeeding) to rid the theater of the artifice and grand theatricality of the nineteenth century.

Rachel was trying to rid the performer (in fact, the human being in general) of his/her hubris and sense of primacy. They could have been mother and daughter—both women theatrical pioneers in their respective generations. Both fueled by a modernist sensibility and a passion for art and for the world.

What is played out in the DbD workshop is the eternal dance between the "I" and the "Other", the negotiations of power, the intermingling of passive and active, the focusing and diffusion of attention, the dialogue between "who I am" and, as Rachel puts it, the "givens" of existence. I came to feel that my education had been backwards; that I had built a lofty roof with Stella, and afterwards the foundation with Rachel.

"Understanding leads to doing" and "Doing by Doing" were both valid concepts but had come in the wrong order.

Rachel has a motto: "There are no mistakes, just bad follow ups". After my initial DbD weekend, I knew that there was much more I needed to learn. I did several more workshops as a participant and many more as a "Slave of Love", Rachel's nickname for her support person. I became a member of the Rachel Rosenthal Company in the early 1990s, performing with the company in original works, written and rehearsed, and in the totally improvised "TOHUBOHU!"

My method of teaching changed radically as a result of this apprenticeship. As adult actors we try to retrain ourselves how to be "in the moment" and act "as if" we are seeing or doing for the first time every time. The beauty of children is that they do—wholeheartedly and without hesitation, and out of that doing understanding comes.

I have been teaching Rachel's method to children and teenagers (in an Arts and Music charter school for three years and now at Espace DbD). I have watched miracles happen every day as a result. Students become more intuitive and aware of their effect on the world around them. Their bodies become articulate, their curiosity and empathy increases. Other teachers have noted their ability to focus on their work despite distractions in the environment. They are adventurous, willing to take risks. They become confident and free. "Be Where You Are Needed" became the mantra for most of my students. Good words to live by.

"Doing by Doing" is a much needed philosophy. Doing music, doing lights, doing sets, moving, using body and voice, improvising—as a soloist, in groups. Being where you are needed in the moment. Art making is soul making. I have been privileged to witness souls being made at Espace DbD for nearly 20 years, for the first time every time. Actors, dancers, poets, painters, surgeons, florists and lawyers have all made wonderful, ephemeral art in this space under the gifted eye of Rachel Rosenthal. Though the weekend is 34 hours long, it is not arduous and taxing, but rather a source of energy and renewal. I continue to do the workshops to this day and learn something new every time.

James Hillman wrote that fear is often the path to calling. He said that to find one's calling, one must set aside the psychological frames that are used because "they don't reveal enough. They trim the life to fit the frame." This has proved true for me. I am grateful every day for the DbD Experience for how it informed and enlarged my life. I hope that this book finds the reader ripe for the experience.

Preface

> "You have to love dancing to stick to it. It gives you nothing back, no manuscripts to store away, no paintings to show on walls and maybe hang in museums, no poems to be printed and sold, nothing but that single fleeting moment when you feel alive. It is not for unsteady souls."
>
> Merce Cunningham

I discovered Merce's quote after having written the following paragraphs. Substitute the words "Total Free Improvisation" for his word "Dance", and the Cunningham message is identical to the Rosenthal message. Not surprisingly!

This book is about theatrical free improvisation. And about the way I teach it. The method that I am about to describe is a resurrection under another name of Instant Theatre, which I created in 1956, and subsequently taught, directed and performed, in a variety of incarnations.

But before you continue to read, let me warn you: You will not get rich if you choose this as your art form. Free improvisation frightens presenters. You may sneak it in during a gig that features a performance piece or several that have been produced, presented, and let's hope, positively reviewed. A free improv can be done at the end of the program perhaps, like an encore in a music recital, a bonus to the venue and its audience, but it's no program header, nor is it something that is well remunerated or financed, and there is no TV or Broadway at the end of the tunnel.

So why do it? In my view, and I have performed in many rehearsed, theatrical, and performance situations, no art form can come close to it in difficulty, in the multimedia aspect of it, in the diversity of its appeal, and also, in its astonishing effect on those who devote themselves to its exigencies and become proficient in and understanding of its demands. Free improvisation makes one better able to sustain a creative, joyous, more fulfilling life, and yes, turns one into a better person! These extravagant assertions are supported by students' post-DbD letters (see Addenda) and are living proof of the truth of my claim!

So this book attempts to give the reader, be she or he a professional artist or not, a glimpse into the space and time needed to train a person in free improvisation, Rosenthal style. I hope that person will be encouraged to pursue this course and find themself on an empowering and magical quest, and, if teaching others, will expose the students to a unique and enthralling ride. The DbD Experience weekend intensive opens the door. Students almost always continue the training with my weekly classes where we explore the form in deeper and more professional ways. But I always ask new students to lay down the base with DbD.

The early "founding" workshops had always been geared to training individuals in the technique I had developed, with the aim of eventually assembling a company of gifted and dedicated players who performed Instant Theatre for adults and, for a time, Instant Fairy Tales for young audiences. It was apparent, however, right from the start, that although my methods brought excellent results in the overt goals, there was evidence of covert side-effects or bonuses that affected the members of the workshops in noticeable ways. People were changing radically as their proficiency in the form progressed, and in ways that altered not only their stage work but also, quite dramatically, their personalities and individual lives. Workshop members reported increased self-awareness and awareness of their environment, altered consciousness, and they began to make radical changes in their personal lives. Some married, others divorced, new careers were embarked on, and lifestyles were overhauled. I accepted these spectacular changes as evidence of the power of the art form and of its influence on human lives. My goal had always been to make art and that priority took precedence over everything else. I was not interested in tailoring my approach to serve psychology or the Growth Movement. When I decided to teach DbD, an abbreviated version of Instant Theatre, I did not alter my approach, but made it available to individuals, both as a theatrical form, and as a personal food for the psyche.

Acknowledgements

There are so many people to thank! First, my publisher, Talia Rodgers, who waited so patiently for this book during decades! Thank you to Kate Noonan, whose feedback is always right on and so useful, and whose moral, physical, and artistic support keeps me going. To Lillian and Jon Lovelace, whose belief in me sustained my art for years. To all my students over the years and decades, who allowed me to develop my vision with them.

A big thank you to my Company members who are joining me in this journey without end, and who appear in the photographs: alexis hunt, Ariadna Rodriguez, C. Derrick Jones, Clint Steinhauser, Craig Ng, Dan Poirier, Doug Hammett, Franc Baliton, Jason Jenn, Joan Spitler, Josue Martinez, Marnie Castor, Michael Morrissey, Mike Steckel, Nathalie Broizat, Nehara Kalev, Pamela Samuelson, Sarnica Lim, Shakuntala Zakheim, Kuva Zakheim, Tad Coughenour and Jarred Cairns. I also thank the many photographers who contributed to this book and also those who remain "unknown" in my memory.

I must also thank those who are no longer close by, but who contributed to my long formation and crystallizing of my method through Instant Theatre and early DbDs: Sally Ann Linton, Lee Mullican, King Moody, Stuart Miller, Sam Weinrib, Sandy Harper, Jerry Harper, Tyan Cyrano, Linda Burnham, Linda Sibio, Sue Dakin, Rochelle Fabb, Michael Sakamoto, Amy Knoles, Stephen Nachmanovitch, Kirk Wilson, etc.

A big thank you to my dear friends Anna Dresdon, Angie Bray, Gilah Hirsch and Rachel Hobreigh for camaraderie forever!

Last but far from least, I wish to thank my companion animals without whom I could not function. These have been most important in my life and work: the Rat Tatti Wattles, the Cats, Kabbalamobile and Batakeeti, and the Company Dogs over the years: Sir Guy, The Fox, Tako, Zatoichi, Hytoo, Barney Bear, Mulan, Cagney, Charlie, Mrs Moore and Sasha the Grand Duke Alexander. Some of my Company members also bring their dogs, and Shade, Tohdoh, Luna, Juju and Scruffles stand out as performers.

And to my shining light, *Merci* to my Cat Dibidi (1954–1972), (she only spoke French), who is my guardian angel on whatever level of being she dwells after her 18-year companionship and inspiration as my living soul mate.

Introduction

Early enough, growing up in Paris, France, I became an artist. Probably by default. Grownups didn't teach me ethics, but mainly manners, languages and the R's. I was never schooled in affairs of the world and its inhabitants, human and non-human. I learned that on my own, over many decades and the hard way. Being an artist was easy. All children would grow to be artists if left alone. I drew, painted, sculpted, visited our bookcases full of wondrous illustrated books, fairy tales from the 1920s and the Victorian era left-over from my older half-sister's early years: the *Thousand and One Nights*, Larousse's large volumes on history, costumes, art, botany, etc. I seldom read but imbibed the illustrations. On Sundays, my father would take me to the Louvre. I was a little girl from an affluent family. We had servants; our car was a Rolls Royce when I was very little, followed by a beautiful Chrysler. That was in the 1920s and 1930s, between the wars, before the War. I had nannies and governesses. I was exposed to my parents and vice versa only at times of maximum grooming, on both sides. We were lovely to each other. On the third floor where I lived, the servants bad-mouthed them and bullied me. The house where I was born was a three-story building with basement that my father had built for my mother. She had a gorgeous contralto voice and sang Russian Gypsy songs accompanying herself on the piano or guitar for intimate audiences of family and friends, in lieu of cabaret patrons who would have been her audience if, as a starving refugee from the Russian Revolution, she had not met my father one cold and snowy Parisian day in January 1921. He was already married and his wife said "No Divorce!" So my mother and father, much in love, lived "in sin", and I was a love child. Father was a dealer in precious stones and oriental pearls, which he caressed lovingly and somewhat erotically on his desk when a new batch arrived from all ends of the world. He also was devoted to the Italian Renaissance and visited all the places where it had flourised, in Italy and elsewhere.

Mara Rosenthal (Rachel's mother), c. 1920. Photographer unknown

He supported a tribal family that he imported from the Russian Caucasus, now Chechnya, and that I met, with much astonishment, only when I was 7 years old, on my birthday, which was the day my parents got officially married (when at last a divorce had been negotiated with wife number 1), and a huge party was given, of the caliber of Maharajah feasts, I imagine. So both were *artistes manqués* and I was to become an artist in their stead.

Growing up with all those silver spoons in my mouth, and learning only how to be a cute and dutiful daughter, it was assumed that I would grow up to be an artist, as very few professional options were open, aside from "good" (meaning rich) marriages, to "girls of good families" in those days.

This assumption stuck but encountered rocky roads when, as a teenager, I began to realize that being an artist and a well-brought-up dutiful daughter was a balancing act hard to keep up. We were Jews, if completely assimilated. I didn't know I was a Jew or what Jews were until much later in life. My father was an atheist, my mother a closet mystic, and I was an atheist like my father who I emulated in every way I could, adored, and wanted to marry.

I am laying out this background to establish that I grew up half spoiled rotten, snobbish, self-centered, willful and male-identified, half neurotically nervous, over-

Leonard Rosenthal (Rachel's father) in his New York office at the Rockefeller Center with pearls, c. 1946. Photographer unknown

Father, Mother and Rachel at the beach in St Jean de Luz, France, 1928. Photographer unknown

sensitive, lonely, confused, and with no skills whatsoever involving human relations, be they over or under our social caste. I thought of myself as an adult masquerading as a child.

My memories as a baby and toddler are of my father mainly, and also of hours spent alone, either in my crib where nannies would let me cry without bringing solace as was the intelligence of the day, or later, playing on my room's floor with a "glass menagerie" that also included silver, ivory, gemstone animals and other precious zoological objects, or architectural blocks, constructing houses, palaces, and exotic mansions with mahjong bricks and wooden fruit trees. Sometimes, my father brought me tiny seed pearls or semi-precious stones, cut or engraved, to play with. All this opulence didn't prevent my growing up with anxiety and fear, as manifested in awful facial tics and nightmares. The Nazis were building their power at that time.

When the war came and my father, my mother and I managed to escape first Paris and then France at the last possible moment, I was 13, looked awkward and what my mother termed in Russian, *kassalapiy*, meaning a version of clumsy, like a dancing bear. I had a big head for my body, and walked pigeon-toed. I had taken ballet lessons but never acquired a good turnout. My hair was "strawberry blond" and golden: my best feature, I would imagine. I was in love with my half-brother Pierre, played with my two nephews, his children, and had no real concept of politics, war, the invasion, or who Nazis were. I had been "sheltered", and was exclusively interested in my own affairs. I drew, created interior decoration made of beach stones during the 1939 "funny war", during which we had escaped the nightly air-raids in Paris by renting yet another villa in St Jean de Luz near the Spanish Pyrenees border where we spent a few months before fleeing France, following all the villas rented there over the years for the lovely summer vacations on the Atlantic shore.

I drew in Spain, I drew in Portugal, I drew in Brazil where we alighted for ten months before finally taking root again in New York City, where my drawing portfolio earned me a place at the High School of Music and Art, just prior to being stolen from the Upper West Side hotel where we were staying upon our arrival from Rio de Janeiro.

I write all this because an artist's life is always very pertinent and people want to know about the formation of that strange creature, the artist, and of his or her talent and work. In my case, my career took off in the late 1940s, early 1950s, and the pull of performance that had been a subtext all along, began to emerge with growing clamor.

Le Cours Fénelon, famous grammar school in the rich district of *Paris Le Seizième Arrondissement*, c. 1934. Rachel in dead center!

Rachel practicing ballet at home in Paris, c. 1932. No turnout! Photographer unknown

I didn't mention performance yet because up to my late teens, I wasn't really aware that it would become my life's work. I was not exposed to much theater or live performance in my early years because "it would make me nervous". I was deprived of a great many things in my childhood because I had been diagnosed as "nervous" and therefore was isolated from other children, the movies, theater, ballet, and, surprisingly, eggs. My father had a very Victorian view of women in theater, and acting was probably the only art form I was not given lessons in before the war, having been briefly exposed to piano, ballet, sculpture, oil painting, and the immobile treasures of the Louvre. After my years at a private grammar school that seems to me in hindsight to have been a throwback to the 1890s, I was tutored by male professors at home. I learned Spanish, my fourth language, after having mastered French (my native language), Russian at 3, and English at 6. I remember little Chekhovian evenings of semi-improvised performances with mother and her friends, and special appearances by "la petite Rachel". I remember doing ballet recitals in our immense living room several years in succession for an audience of 100–150 family members and friends on the occasion of my birthdays, choreographed by Olga Preobrajenska, my teacher and teacher of ballet stars. I recall the excruciating fear and excitement, the endless delicious fittings of dreamy tutus created by Karinska, costumer to ballet stars, the feeling of utter failure because I could already tell an imposter from the real thing, and finally, in the last of those recitals, the shame and embarrassment before my partner, a young boy hired from Madame Preo's class, already viewed as a future star, and his obvious superiority as a dancer. No matter. I soldiered on, and was elated. There was *applause*, people who courted my parents—and there were many—complimented me, and I went upstairs to go to bed, surrounded with presents, waiting for my mother to come and kiss me goodnight. Proustian, no?

I was by nature an improviser. In high school, in English class, I improvised a scene from a literary play with so much success that my teacher begged me to join the Dramatic Club after class hours. Knowing how my father felt, I refused. Repeatedly. For my teacher asked me time and again, even finally kneeling before me to beg me to join. Really. Since I was dying to anyway, I finally accepted. I was in a play, a *commedia* called *Aria Di Capo* by Edna St Vincent Millay, and it was discovered that I had no vocal projection whatsoever. My costume and movements were swell, but, in the big auditorium, you couldn't hear a word I said. After desperate attempts at augmenting my volume and failing miserably, I suffered the humiliation of having to recite most of my lines standing by a mike. Not having mike technique training, I went in and out of hearing. Awful. Shame. Abomination. Regret.

I concentrated on visual arts after that fiasco. I was awarded the Gold Medal of Art on graduation, felt the sting of envy and outrage from some students, and went into the world, determined to break through the oil painting barrier that had been my Achilles heel all along. I studied with Hans Hoffman, Karl Knaths and Morris Davidson, and discovered that my obstacle to becoming a good painter was not necessarily lack of talent; it was a block toward understanding and dealing with Time. My comfort, right from the start, had been in creating an improvised, one-time-only invention that my energy and inspiration carried brilliantly in the moment, whether the object was visual art or theatrical performance. But afterwards, I couldn't tolerate the time alone, in the studio or wherever, learning, *practicing* (hooo! that awful word!), rehearsing, and progressing . . . I didn't have the discipline, the rigor, the drive, the mindset, for that necessary component of any art form. I could only dash through a drawing, a calligraphy, a dramatic improv . . . and be done with it. Off to something else. And so that's what I did, unaware of the true nature of this skill, always denigrating and dumping on myself while feeling superior to everyone else. Harder to do than you might think!

Throughout my early years, I had a vague intuition that something fabulously wonderful was just around the corner, and that if I could just turn that corner, I would "live the good life". What was "the good life"? At that time I read Henry James' novella *The Beast in the Jungle*: a man spends his life feeling that a "beast" will eventually pounce on him, some amazing event that would single him out in the world. He waits for that beast to pounce all his life, and just before dying he comes to the realization that the "beast" had already pounced, and that he would be the only person on Earth to whom *nothing would ever happen*! That story scared the bejeezus out of me and I did all in my power all my life to prevent *that* beast from pouncing!

In the late 1940s, I studied in Paris at the EPJD (Education Par le Jeu Dramatique), Jean-Louis Barrault's school of theater, taught by the most avant-garde (Roger Blin) as well as the most classical (actors from the Comédie-Française), and people in between (such as Tania Balachova). But the classes I loved best were Improv with a guy whose name I forget, who was a psychologist and not a theater person at all. It was during this time that I made a discovery that changed my life. After all the years of ping-ponging between visual art and theater, and with the prodding of Daniel Emilfork and Denise Peron, my buddies at the EPJD, I read Antonin Artaud's *Le Théâtre et son double*, later translated into English by M.C. Richards in New York, another buddy from a subsequent period. Artaud's book totally amazed and enchanted me. He was presenting me with the solution to my problem. He posited an art form that was neither all literary, nor all visual art, a way of integrating all the arts under one banner, thus allowing me to indulge in all the art forms that I loved and that I feared had turned me into a dilettante, because I couldn't decide on just one to be my life's work. I could use Music, Poetry, Lighting, Sets, Costuming, all

Performative Arts such as Acting, Mime, Acrobatics, and Dance, as well as Painting, Film, Projections, etc. It was intoxicating and I finally knew where I was going, although it was still a while before I could turn this realization into concrete work.

Back in New York City, I enrolled in the Dramatic Workshop directed by Erwin Piscator. He had been evicted from Germany and his communism made trouble for him in the United States as well. But he had a good school, pushed his Brechtian "Epic" theater, while also incubating the future "Method", taught by Lee Strasberg, pre-Actor Studio. I became Piscator's assistant, and also the assistant of the main set designer, Heinz Condell. Everyone passed through Piscator's gate including Brando (the class just before mine), as well as people like Tony Franciosa and Ben Gazzara, both of whom I directed in their first stage performance. I did good work there because continental style was somewhat favored. At least by Piscator and most of the professors who were European refugees like me. And, I improvised.

I spent eight post-war years doing what I now realize was the major component of my then personality: leaping back and forth between two continents, never staying long enough to catch up with myself, not going into any depth in my learning, improvising my life, astonishing people in one city only to leave before they became disenchanted with my shallowness and disabused by my bravado. My life was structured as an improv: all the energy spent on one target, filled with inspiration, instant instinct, theatrical derring-do, sudden finds, and then the return, the realization that I was only a channel, a conduit for something volatile and ephemeral that I didn't have the courage, patience or know-how to pursue, and that could abandon me any time without my being able to call it back. I lived from ecstasy to dread, unable to pinpoint my malaise, marching into the full sunlight with aplomb and then retreating like a spider into my cave. This malaise haunted me for more than half my life.

I spent three years in a downtown New York loft, with the friendship of John Cage, Merce Cunningham, Bob Rauschenberg, Cy Twombly and Jasper Johns among others. That was the period when all these young men and their entourage (of which I was part) were discovering their relationships to each other, as well as their relationships to their talents and arguably, genius. That was before 1955. Bob discovered his Combines, Jap (Jasper Johns) discovered his encaustic targets and flags, John and Merce, deep into Zen Buddhism, created dance companies and developed their art philosophies. I carried some of those ideas and notions with me to California, as well as a sizable precious collection of these artists' works of that period.

Having been close to those artists for a few years, and still unsure and tentative about what I myself had to offer, I was naturally overwhelmed by their originality and the aplomb with which they broke rules and established themselves as pioneers in a new art world, local and global, that was eventually transformed by the radiation of their sensibility.

Jasper Johns "Jap", 1953. Photo by Robert Rauschenberg

Bob Rauschenberg and Jap in Jap's loft on Pearl Street, one floor below Rachel's, 1954. Photo by Rachel Rosenthal

View of Rachel's loft on Pearl Street with works by Jap, Bob, and Cy Twombly, 1955. Photos by Rachel Rosenthal

Of course, they dazzled me, and when I left for Los Angeles in 1955, I brought within me influences that I wasn't even totally aware of.

In Los Angeles, I was hired by the Pasadena Playhouse to teach something they called "dramatic dance". I taught "dramatic dance", or my interpretation of it, mostly improvisation, and I directed a few plays and a demonstration piece to tour and recruit students for the school. I had no inkling as to how to teach, never having done it. But I had an instinct for it and the students liked my freedom (and theirs). However, the very conservative Playhouse infrastructure did not appreciate me at all. I didn't wear the right clothes, and (this was not stated but was obvious), they thought I was too sexual (I taught African dance). I was asked to resign when the semester ended. Shocked and saddened at first, I soon found a small box theater, adjacent to Hollywood's Circle Theater, and began to teach workshops there. The year was 1956.

I enrolled young students, and would-be starlets in the industry. Vic Morrow, Tony Perkins, Tab Hunter and others passed through our doors. They presented the usual scene study that bored me no end. When they hadn't done their homework and had nothing prepared, I had them do exercises that I invented while in a twilight zone between waking and napping on my bed in the afternoon. Those exercises were the start of my "method" that I've been honing ever since.

I was poor in those days and completely unschooled in the art of making a living. Most of my students "forgot" to pay tuition, and I forgot to ask. But my little theater and its product had a rich sheen to it, albeit made with nothing and less-than-nothing. The lessons of Bob and Jap's collages and assemblages, created with detritus for the most part (the allure of garbage!), were not lost on me. John's "silences" too, and Merce's hauteur regarding the place of music within his dance compositions. I soon realized that the stage could be a Paul Klee, a Schwitters, a "Mille Fleurs" tapestry, or a light-suffused color-field painting, all done with a minimum of means, yet all vibrant, atmospheric, emotively delineated, and esthetically transporting. We obtained these effects with finds in back alleys before the garbage truck passed, as people threw away treasures since garage sales hadn't yet been invented. We gathered bits and pieces, paper goods, cardboard boxes, old clothes, debris from house-wrecks, etc. We had no theatrical lights, but used gelled clamp-ons, carried by the performers in their hands, fluidly "painting" the scene with moving shafts of color, modest precursors of the psychedelic lighting that revolutionized stagecraft later on.

I sometimes put on a long-playing record (LP) and just let the actors live out their esthetic and their tales for the length of the record. The lighting people were on stage with the performers, moving slowly and carefully, in tune with the action, harmonizing with their movements, sometimes in "close-up", sometimes further out in space, at times entering the audience area to flood the stage with a wide

Instant Theatre postcard designed by Rachel Rosenthal, 1963

beam. I had painted the little black box white, an action that Peter Brook performed for *A Midsummer's Night Dream* years later to great pomp and fanfare! The various clamp-ons with their saturated color gels created wonderfully shaped and tinted shadows all around the white ceiling and walls. We brought in found objects of all sorts, branches and flowers, and created objects of our own, strange contraptions that emerged from assembling bric-a-brac. We used them in abstract ways, transforming them into ritual objects of mystery and power. We moved like dancers, like acrobats, like animals, like rocks. We used our voices and whatever gibberish seemed appropriate. As I sat there in the dark, watching this hour or so of enthralling theater art—people defying gravity on high ladders, in a trance, with no fear, metamorphoses of humans into strange beasts, using bodies, masks and props like sorcerers, like shamans, sometimes drumming and improvising live music with the collection of sound and noise-makers we had accumulated, I realized that we were approximating Artaud's theatrical vision. There it was, before my very eyes as I sat propped on cushions strewn over the bleachers denuded of chairs. Theater of Cruelty, of the Absurd . . . the real thing! I was agape! We had really created something new and fabulous. What we had was magic, fairy tales for adults, dance but not-dance, painting but not-painting, a new world of art such as I had never before experienced. And it was a one-time-only precious art-time, never repeated and never-to-be-seen beyond that inspired first time! In Paris, at that time, Jean-Louis Barrault called his work "Total Theater". I called mine *Instant Theatre*. The name was a mix of the newly invented "instant" coffee—a nod toward Pop art—and Zen!

Instant Theatre was a totally spontaneous and collective theatrical form. We created, not only the stage action—which involved text, movement, dance, mime, a sophisticated *mise-en-scène* that could be described as a mix of Ridiculous Theater, Theater of Images, Performance Art, Theater of the Absurd, Theater of Cruelty, and Cabaret—but also sets, lights, sound, music and costumes, during each piece. We believed the unbelievable: that a fully realized, richly theatrical production could be presented with no preconception whatsoever, no director, no script, no light plot, no cues! And once this feat had been accomplished, we were perfectly willing to drop it, never to recapture or repeat it, and blithely turned our attention to the next piece that crystallized out of thin air!

It was insane. But logically born from my immersion in Zen Buddhism, my closeness to Merce Cunningham, John Cage, Bob Rauschenberg and Jasper Johns, my enthusiasm over Antonin Artaud's writings, and my firm belief that we could do everything, know everything, and bring out of ourselves whatever was required for the feat.

In the beginning, after some relaxation exercises, the stage action would start as in a dream, by one person joined presently by others, each one enriching the initial action either by enhancement or collision, like the slow building up of a painting, layer by layer. At first the form was very amorphous, very permissive, and almost always yielded, when allowed to last an hour or so, some grandiose friezes or frescoes of Boschian or Jungian imagery, as well as individual psychological residue. Those early sessions were so overwhelming that I sat there transfixed, almost afraid to breathe, thinking how privileged I was to witness the performance, like some secret primeval mystery and sacred rite, never to be seen again, never recorded, gone forever as I sat there, ephemeral and infinitely beautiful!

After a few such sessions, I brought the group together and told them how I felt. I added, "We must go public!" At which point, nearly all my students disappeared. Their reason: "My agent wouldn't want me to be seen in something so weird!"

Only three people were left: a painter (the wonderful Lee Mullican), a dancer who had been my student at Pasadena Playhouse (then called Sally Ann Linton), and an MIT engineering student from India. So we were four. One or two people joined us later on, but my project of total improvisation was daunting to most, and I had few takers at first for public shows. The four of us workshopped all week, hours on end, and opened our doors to the public on weekends. Our first audience was made up of the artists who exhibited at the Ferus Gallery: Wally Berman, Ed Kienholtz, Billy Al Bengston, John Altoon, with assorted wives and girlfriends, the

Lee Mullican in Instant Theatre, Hollywood 1956. Photo by Rachel Rosenthal

director of the Ferus, Walter Hopps, a young man called George Herms, who to this day credits Instant Theatre for having steered him in his art path with our visuals and treatment of objects! These people attracted others, notably the habitués of Samson de Brier's Salon (Anaïs Nin was one of them), and any celebrity and visual or cinematic artist who came through Los Angeles, all of who alighted invariably at Samson's. It was a very tight group, very elite, very cliquey and bohemian, very Paris-in-the-1920s. Very Hollywood. We presented a different program every night, totally improvised, sometimes esoteric and abstract, sometimes pastiches of realistic theater, and everything in between. People lounged on the cushions, smoking pot, and I, very ignorant in these matters, had no notion of that happening. Our spectators "grooved" on the stage event, were high, and extremely receptive to everything we did! So of course, I believed we were extraordinary and unbeatable, and we probably were, floating on a cloud of marijuana! I've since wondered if the others in the company were aware, but I never asked. It was long ago, and I do believe the work stood on its own merits, albeit enhanced in ecstatic brains!

There were long pieces that unfolded like butterfly wings out of a cocoon. It might begin in darkness. Perhaps a faint metallic rap is heard, or a clash of cymbals. Or a rainfall from a sound effect record. A spot of red light scans the stage area, with a golden glow descending from above, creating a giant shadow. From somewhere, a rhythmic breathing is heard, and a muffled call. The lights intensify, silhouetting some strong spatial planes delineated by tension lines of elastic tape pulled tightly in diagonals across the stage. A panel of Mylar catches the changing lights and reflects the shape of a player, cocoon-like in a long jersey tube stretched out of shape by objects that envelop the player within, giving him, it, a strange prehistoric animal look. Three other players enter, in a tight unit, moving and speaking in precise unison. The piece continues, protean, as players enter and exit, as the moods shift with the colored lights, the tone of the instruments, the rhythm of the movements, the texture of the words. The content is sometimes precise, analytical, funny, sometimes impressionistic and dream-like. The piece becomes an entity, with a life of its own, different from all the others, with individual theme, look, feel, meaning, and life span. It ends the way an organism dies, when its life is spent, with every part sensing the end and contributing to its conclusion. It can be profoundly moving, even enlightening, but difficult to analyze, the way dreams are. To an audience it can be challenging and exciting. To the participants, exhilarating. Players feel they have somehow been "beside themselves", transported beyond their limits. They either moved in ways they never had before, or spoke on subjects they knew nothing about and did so eloquently, or performed music in an inspired way. Even if their contribution to the piece was minimal, they felt a part of a mysterious and bewitching process, a kind of communal birth, a becoming.

Lee Mullican and others in Instant Theatre, Hollywood 1956. Photo by Rachel Rosenthal

Instant Theatre number 1 ended, and there was a long suite of Instant Theatres after that. I met King Moody in 1958, we married in 1960, and having created new workshops, I had a growing number of performers that I groomed and developed for about nine months before exposing them slowly to the exigencies of improvising in front of an audience. We were always broke, and performed and taught in various modest spaces: tiny theaters, garages, dance studios, lofts. We ended up giving spectacles in our own home, a rickety, cantilevered "bungalow" in Laurel Canyon (the Hollywood Hills), that people accessed by parking their cars high up the hill and walking down a quarter of a mile or so, only to climb three stories to sit on old car seats or cushions on the floor, to see us doing our thing with a sheet hiding the kitchen, and with our inevitable clamp-on lights. But this time, they were plugged into a homemade light board, with dimmers. We had evolved in our style, with more speaking, influenced by King, who had a theatrical schooling background from New York. When we couldn't accommodate the growing audience, we decided to go professional. In 1963 we rented the little Horseshoe Stage Theater (now called the Zephyr) on Melrose Avenue. We added weekend shows for children that were also improvised but with a fairy-tale storyline, calling it Instant Fairy Tales. The childrens shows paid the rent, and were a delight to perform.

Rachel with husband and partner King Moody in Instant Theatre at the Horseshoe Stage Theater, Hollywood (now called The Zephyr) 1964. Photographer unknown

And so we played, always deepening our understanding of an art form that we were probably alone in practicing, too poor to spend on documentation—thus cheating posterity of our work—and developing a solid following of people for whom our theater was a secret little magic space that they visited on weekends, knowing that there would never be two evenings alike, marveling at our successes and crestfallen at our failures along with us, always supportive and amazed, willing to gamble the low price of admission in hope of an evening of wonders.

Rachel in *The Death Show*, an early solo performance, Space Gallery, Hollywood 1978. Photo by David Moreno

We closed in 1966 because I suffered from degenerative arthritis of the knees, and could no longer move the way I wanted. There came a long hiatus of nine years during which I concentrated on visual arts, exhibited my clay sculptures, and moved to the Valley with King and a quantity of dogs and cats that were in danger of death on Laurel Canyon tributaries that had become like car-race tracks. I performed my first performance art solo in 1975, we revived Instant Theatre briefly in 1976–1977, and lost our shirts because we had unknowingly rented a nice theater that was adjacent to the Red Light district, and the parents wouldn't bring their children to that neighborhood!

The seeming death of Instant Theatre precipitated the death of our marriage, and King and I separated and later divorced. I moved back to Los Angeles, and recreated myself again as a solo performer, this time presenting pieces long on text, rehearsed and performed multiple times—the opposite of Instant Theatre. I became known as a "performance artist", having assimilated several performance art approaches along with feminism, but I was still very theatrical and therefore not a bona fide performance artist. I fell into the cracks in terms of categorization, but that was nothing new. I could never be categorized in my long life and career! I enjoyed a good 25-year run, with the satisfaction of recognition, awards, grants, and touring gigs on three continents.

In 1979, two friends who had been members of Instant Theatre, Sandy Harper and Tyan Cyrano, urged me to devise weekend workshops of the IT (Instant Theatre) technique. EST (Erhard Seminars Training) was very popular then, and was emulated at the time by other groups. I had a great deal of resistance to that notion. I taught IT for months before seeing any real understanding or progress in my students, and they stayed because they trusted me and had a living, visual experience of the ultimate goal of their travail, as they watched our weekend shows. I couldn't conceive of squeezing this development into a weekend and finding any satisfaction, either for me or for my students. They kept up the pressure. I knew I had to find a way of earning a living, and I knew that I had no other skills than the technique I had developed over the last decades. So I plunged in.

At first there was the business of attracting students. I had many contacts due to my involvement with the feminist art movement in Los Angeles in the first part of the seventies. I already had a modest following who came to my performances. So I offered my services free for the first few weekends, hoping that, if things went well, those people would suggest that their friends take my workshop too, which is what happened. But there was the question of a name. I didn't want to call it Instant Theatre, as that was not what it was. After much deliberation, I ended up with a name that sounds jolly and that describes the work very well: The DbD Experience, DbD standing for "Doing by Doing". DbD also stands for something else, close to my heart, and you will read what it is at the end of this book!

I move into my building, ESPACE DBD on South Robertson Blvd, Los Angeles, 1980. Photo by Rachel Rosenthal

What is Doing by Doing?

As developed over three decades at this writing, the workshop is many things to different people. For some students it is a weekend of fun and games, others want to overcome certain fears associated with performing, some people wish to discover things about themselves, others need to deepen their existing theatrical skills, and finally some hope to transform their lives. Amazingly enough, most people find what they seek. Over the years, few people have left before the end, or had a strong aversion to what was happening. I can count such situations on the fingers of one hand. For the most part, expectations are met and fulfilled, and the effect of the weekend on individuals seems to continue well beyond those two and a half days. Some "awakenings" have been wondrous!

I had witnessed the powerful effect of Instant Theatre on students in the past. I remember, for example, a young boy who enrolled for private lessons. He used to lie down on stage while I created a set and played a long LP of music. He sometimes stayed prone on the floor for most of his allotted hour. Suddenly he'd jump up, and in the few minutes left, feverishly begin to rearrange the set until he had created a cemetery! This he did no matter what the set represented or suggested. After many such sessions, I was inspired to create a cemetery set for starters. When I did, he remained lying on the floor for the duration of the hour and didn't budge. When he came for his next session, I created another kind of set, and he didn't start by lying down.

He spent the whole hour dancing in ways he had never moved before, exotic, sensual, and beautiful. He didn't come back! I was dumbfounded and realized then the magical power of this theatrical approach, both in instilling art and enabling psychological transformation.

DbD is an intensive weekend that lasts 34 hours, sometimes more. In that time, the students hear three talks by me, do group movement meditations, exercises that address different theatrical issues, as solos, duets and groups, small and large; do voice work; receive training in lighting, music, set making, costuming and use of props. An assignment is given on Friday night and presented on Saturday afternoon. Improvisations are performed throughout, with or without themes, and forms are learned to create strong structures. On Sunday, along with more exercises, we attempt the culmination of the learned art form, with free improvisations, including a long group improv we call a Rambler. Throughout the weekend, large improvised group choreographies are performed, using techniques learned and instant discoveries. Sunday night, a drumming circle terminates the three sessions.

Nothing mysterious or magical in any of that. Yet the results certainly are. Why?

I attribute the effects of the DbD Experience to several causes. The primary ones are the states of desire, of high expectation, and of trust. There is a big wish to be fulfilled, entering this arena. And the natural states of attention, willingness, and hope are powerful engines during the three days. People are eager to be bowled over, to be transported, to be swept off their feet. In the past, the so-called "Growth Movement" prepared students to submit themselves to exercises designed for personal enlightenment. It was ubiquitous, and individuals and groups sprouted everywhere in pursuit of transformation, either as teachers or learners. Nowadays, we live in an atmosphere of speed, competition, anxiety and fear. We need to succeed at all costs, preferably before the other guy. The letters I receive from students written pre-DbD betray these states, and therefore the people are both ready for the fulfillment of high expectations, and anxious that they may be disappointed. Some people and their letters are "cool", but it soon becomes apparent in the work that they are simply more dissimulated. At that juncture of their emotional crossroad, it is important to create an atmosphere of trust, ease, safety, excitement, and acceptance, to combat the inner critic while entrusting the students with techniques that are almost foolproof for ensuring success. The more people succeed, the more confident they become, the more willing to accept their success and build on it. The exercises are not easy. But relaxation and trust make their success achievable. It is a very positive process and one that can be viewed with simplicity or complexity, but either way, atmosphere, a certain rhythm in the curriculum, confidence in self and others, shedding of preconceived and negative attitudes, and enjoyment in the art form itself, are all necessary ingredients to create a fertile ground for art, and for laying the foundation of a more satisfying, fruitful and joyful personal life.

Early on, I tell the students to avoid nudity and sado-masochism, and that the use of any animals is strictly forbidden. I remind them that performance art has a long track record of the above, including the many uses of food and the introduction of body secretions and fluids. These are now performance clichés and should be avoided, mostly on the grounds of "been there, done that"! I have no moral grounds for limiting these uses, except for the animal issue. For the rest, such as nudity or any blood-letting, etc., I object to these repeated motifs and clichés that have had ample exposure, and feel that violence and brutality can be portrayed by metaphor, and that inventiveness and originality in the use of nudity is a must. Such imagery cannot be used for shock value any more because we've been shocked and over-shocked! If you are to strip, it should be for a darn good reason! Shocking an audience is not half as interesting or important as touching an audience.

The training works as follows: it gives permission to the individuals to discover themselves, to be more profoundly who they are, to dig into deep and unknown areas of being and express what they find through their instrument—body and voice. It can open the gates of creativity in the direction of one's life work, fulfilling aspirations in art, or any other work that is in line with who that person is and what their highest aspiration leads them to do.

At no time should the work be confused with psychodrama or group therapy. Since there is very little discussion, that danger is easily avoided. The tendency to fall into self-indulgence must be stopped, nipped in the bud. The focus, at all times, is on art making. Relationships are not based on personality but on energy. People's different energies become the motor for art making, and relationships are based on individual needs for achieving certain artistic ends. The fact that people must rotate between performing and doing the so-called "technicals" (sound/music, sets, lights), helps to put people on an equal level at the same time as turning them into "Renaissance men and women". Watch for those who try to sneak out of doing lights, or sets, or whatever, with the lame excuse that "they don't want to spoil the performance"!

So what exactly is Doing by Doing? It is precisely what it says it is. You learn, you accomplish, you evolve, not by theorizing but by concretizing. Ideas and concepts are the backbone of the work. But they must be transmuted into matter, into something sensorily perceptual. It must be felt, seen, touched, heard, not just thought. Physically. Ideas alone don't promote growth. They can drag you into standing water, and give you a false image of yourself, a narcissistic view of a self-portrait that is in reality a still life. You are what you do, and what you do impacts the environment, which, in turn, impacts you. If concepts and ideas remain in your head, if they are not translated into the duress of concretizing, of making, of doing, they go nowhere, and neither do you. So the mystery, the secret of DbD's success is that, for two and a half full days, you are doing, doing, doing, bringing to light your innermost impulses and fantasies, your feelings, your uniqueness and total being. You are then able to perceive the gestalt, and can shape it further in any way you wish. You also get a sense of its effect on others. It is an "In and Out" process that sets a whole gamut of dynamics in motion. Hence changes in one's life, in one's thinking, in one's doing.

What sorts of things emerge from the DbD work? Have they been hidden from view for a reason? Are they dangerous? I said earlier that we know everything, and can do anything. Human beings are an encyclopedia of knowledge, an Alexandrian library where all is stored. As fetuses, we experience in nine months what it took evolution millions of years to accomplish. Our brains contain the brains of animal evolution, from reptilian to lower mammalian, to human. We "remember" our history in our genes and cells. These things are available to us, if we allow them to surface. The process of art is like archeology with ourselves as the digging sites. But our senses have developed in such a way as to filter a great deal of our environment. We don't hear along the complete spectrum of sound. We don't see along the complete spectrum of sight. To have the whole capacity of hearing and seeing would be chaotic and would tax our brains to insanity. Irrelevant external stimuli are screened and filtered out by stern internal censors in order to keep our sanity intact. If these censors are deranged, madness results.

So, do we want to open the doors of the "library"? Is it safe?

We are blessed with a wonderful consciousness, and an equally wonderful subconscious. Somehow, unless there is illness, our brains are capable of dredging up material that can be revelatory, but short of destructive. Using psyche-altering substances is dangerous for that reason. These chemicals destroy the censors and may, indeed, be extremely destructive to the functions of the brain. There is no chaos in DbD. The discoveries are benign. They may touch upon memory, but mostly they deal with form. Ways of moving. Ways of using voice. Ways of creating spaces and rhythms that were never experienced before. Ways of entering slight trances that allow the channeling of stage events that create their own harmonies and astonishing effects. A way of composing on our feet, words, actions, relationships with living beings and objects that transform their meaning and their use. Ways of manipulating space and time. All of these things are indeed benign, but also extremely powerful. The exaltation of feeling capable of bringing the impossible to light is intoxicating.

Improvisational performance and its relationship to life

DbD training functions much like our living reality. In this lies its effectiveness as a teaching tool. No matter how abstract or absurd the performance material may appear on the surface, the underlying principles are the same as those of our lives.

Group unit forms in an improv. Photo by Kate Noonan

A DbD performance consists of a confluence of events whose sum and interaction shape the space–time continuum from moment to moment and is, in turn, shaped by it. The same is true of our daily existence. The totality of a performance's components becomes the stage reality in the same way that the unfolding of our being is the result of myriad forces, events, fields, and actions of which we are aware only to a limited degree. Life is a hugely complex dance that boasts not one but an infinite number of choreographers. Each present moment is a constellation of things conscious and unconscious, and is determined by individuals, groups, social forces, environment, ecology, weather, the past, the future, and by "accidents" that are the unexpected interference of events engendered far from the "theater of operation", like comets coming at us from the depth of space. Our conscious grasp or control of these things is limited. We are never totally in charge just as we are never totally victimized by it. We are active and passive at the same time. All is fluidity, a give and take, an in and out, action and reaction, simultaneous, in flow and flux, just happening, happening, happening. And with the result of making art.

To conclude: why is The DbD Experience such an influence on people's lives? I believe that it impacts one very strongly and intimately because it is based on the same principles as our evolution as human beings. To put it simply, it works the way evolution works, and the way life is expressed in our being. We respond to actions, events, the unexpected, by a process that is akin to improvisational performance, the only difference is that, in our lives, the process is continuous, whereas in the making of art, it is discontinuous and "in brackets", so to speak. In other words, we make art at times, but live our lives all the time.

Still, the process is similar. We are alive. We are born, live and die. This alone is totally remarkable and miraculous. The fact of our Planet of Life is *the* sacred fact in our consciousness, and whether we explain it scientifically, religiously, or by a mix of both, it nevertheless is *the* most important element in what we do, know, and are. Therefore, we must keep aware of the miracle of Life, whether in our approach to art making, or our experience of daily and moment-by-moment living. Free improvisation allows us to feel what that's like and enables us to retain this capacity in or out of the theater.

From what we now know, life began on this planet as part of a continuum of chemical processes at the bottom of the sea. It seems possible that the first organisms appeared at the places of lava eruption in the depth of oceans, of extreme heated vents that somehow, in ways unknown to us at this point, nurtured live, replicating organisms. These unicellular beings replicated at first by division, one cell splitting into two, thus populating the bottom of the sea rather quickly. Eventually however, the unicellular beings united, forming multicellular organisms,

"Two cells dividing" (free improv). Photographer unknown

and differentiation entered the picture, with discrete organs being created by different cells. At that juncture, division was no longer possible, and the food chain began, and with it sex, death, and the predator/prey combo.

Amazingly enough, two distinct forms of life branched out: the vegetal and the animal. And even more amazingly, evolution, albeit taking its time, didn't stop there, but, pressed forward by climate changes and chemical transformations, it burst into a mind-boggling array of living forms that were only the first step in the continuous and extraordinary journey of the populating of Earth.

Evolution is a mystery. The way it functions is so completely akin to art-making as to be the template for our cultural evolution.

I don't think that evolution would have existed without the advent of Play. We humans began our cultural history by playing. In that we were not alone. Animals of all sorts have played and are playing, creating dances, games, songs, body decorations and object arrangements of all kinds, all useful to their lives and reproduction. There is no reason to think that we did not perform the same functions. To all these animal art forms, we also added language, bringing more specificity and variety to forms of communication that had already been in use among other animals. Baby animals play, preparing them for adulthood activities, birds attract the opposite sex by making art of objects collected or architectural structures, monkeys color themselves evolutionarily in bright hues, etc. Even the simplest organisms are aware and conscious, and try to avoid predators with ingenious camouflage. Some of these "games" are a question of life and death, but seeing the esthetically intricate choreographies of fish schools and bird flocks, one cannot escape the perception of play and/or art, and many animal games seem to exist solely for pleasure.

Art, games, play, are all associated with the physical. They promote good feelings that our brains identify as Pleasure. Nowadays however, a new imperative has entered, and that is Economics. We all want to feel good but few of us experience pleasure in satisfying quantity, in our daily lives. Art has now been hijacked by Economics. Still, there is something special and unique about the making of art, the connection with the unconscious, with the creative field of Earth, with the satisfaction that comes from bringing forth something that didn't exist before, and none of these things are related to economics! Art is one of the few remaining unadulterated pleasures in life! Pleasure is an imperative of Life, and it isn't always available in our present civilization in spite of the billions we spend on it. Entertainment seems to give pleasure, but is often no more than distraction from worries and sadness. Sex may give pleasure but cannot be a continual source. Sport is pleasurable but vicarious, and we, more often than not, pay others a great deal of money to play instead of us. The passion with which we identify with those who do our "playing" is proof of the importance of that sort of pleasure in our lives. The feelings that

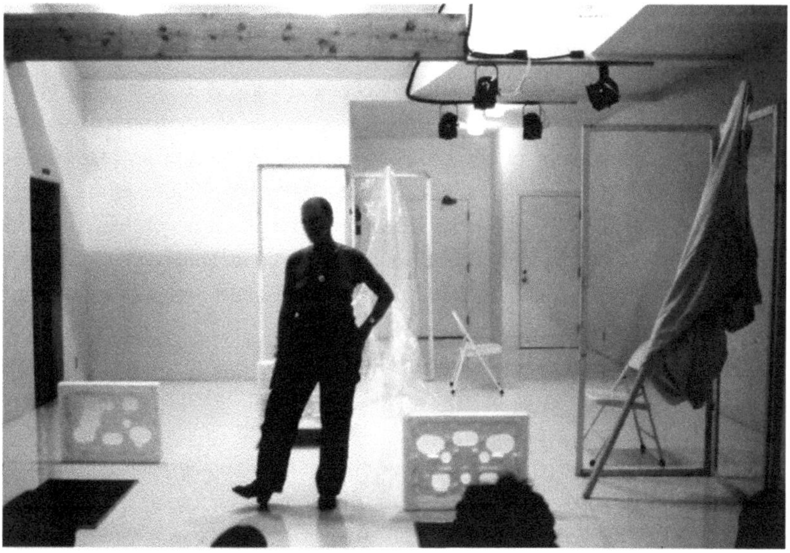

Rachel giving feedback in set demo. Photographer unknown

play and/or art give rise to are intricately connected to the miracle of Life and Evolution. They are therefore sacred. The sense of awe, of the sacred, that trees give, that a baby of any species gives, that images of Earth, either from space or on her surface, give, are like those of making fabulous art or viewing it. It catches the breath, it elevates. You have participated! Alas, those pleasures are so often adulterated by very alien concerns: finances, criticism, scarcity, competition, prestige, trophies, status.

Even with structure and routine, we are constantly expected to meet events that come our way. They can be totally unexpected or, if expected, the form they adopt may be surprising and new. In the DbD workshop, such is the way we also make art. Stimuli of all sorts alight in our path. We deal with everything, sometimes consciously and make fast choices, sometimes impulses and reflexes happen without our conscious decision-making. We respond to visible and invisible occurrences: the air, gravity, timing, sounds, mood, other performers, objects, accidents, etc. Just as we do in "real" life! Only, because it's "art", we deem it more precious and are more receptive and aware than we would be in our mostly unconscious daily experiences.

Writing the DbD book

It is important to give a dry and matter-of-fact description of the DbD, in order to appreciate, as we go into details, the astonishing power of the experience. I have hesitated to write about it for decades because I realized the difficulty of translating that experience into language. Language is not a part of the DbD method, except for a few words allowed on Sunday. To deprive people of language is to unlock the floods of body-centered knowledge and action that often defers to words. Words can be crutches, and using none forces imagination, energy, and invention that lie dormant when language is allowed to take over. Rehashing the past in any form bores me. It also invites reliving the anxiety that haunted me for such a long time. I hate to talk about what "happened", I love what "is happening". I teach as if channeling, reacting and dealing with what is before me. I absorb the moment of experiencing a student or a piece, work with that tangible fragment of time, with what a student is expressing and sending out, responding and reacting to that student as a cause and effect phenomenon. I don't use knowledge acquired yesterday. Or lessons learned. I must be able to sense the ways in which the student is different and unique and help the individual shape and sculpt that persona, that personal artistry, to become a better artist. I can't do that on my own, or self-consciously. I can only be effective when I let knowledge and wisdom flow through me.

Just as happens in a good improv, one day, as I was ready to email some friends, my fingers began to dance on the keyboard and write the book, and they haven't stopped. I let them, trusting that the fingers knew something I didn't know. When something like that happens, when one part of the body imperatively demands something, the rest of the body checks to see if it's good for the rest or not, and then the brain decides whether to go along or not, other considerations playing into it. In this case, I didn't hesitate and let the fingers tap! So here I am, facing the hardest task that ever befell me, and enjoying every moment of it!

More about DbD

In the DbD Experience I propose that we know all there is to know at this time, if we are willing to listen—to our bodies, to our consciousness and our conscience, to the Earth, to the Cosmos. We are, after all, made up of these things, and since we are, we have been programmed to have access, on the cellular level, to Cosmos, Earth, consciousness, body. To gain this access, we need the key, the Open Sesame of silence, focus, trust, listening, and a vehicle. That vehicle is art. I believe that all arts are fundamentally alike and possess the ability to plug us into the above-

"Two performers in a tube, confronted by Frog" (free improv). Photographer unknown

mentioned knowledge. But theatrical improvisation seems to be the most profound, rapid, and effective art form to achieve this connection, as I have experienced it over the decades. DbD is designed to achieve that state in record speed and with lasting benefits.

Letters

The DbD Experience begins when a student agrees to do the weekend, and we ask her or him to send a letter telling us who they are, anything they wish to share about their background or their life, and what they want to get out of the workshop. These letters are very important. I don't necessarily remember the details, but I remember the feeling they give. What paper they use, what their writing looks like, whether they spell correctly, how long or short the letter, what other materials are sent, the emotional subtext of their content, all expose their sender. I have found, over the years, several recurring concerns, fear being the most often expressed. What is this fear? Mostly it involves the unknown: "Who am I? What will I find out about myself? I will be exposed, and found to be lacking, inadequate; I will be shamed . . ." People who have never faced an audience fear that. People who have, and have bad memories of it, fear that. People who are competitive fear not being "first" and "best". People who are shy fear exposure. People who believe I will be stern, difficult, demanding, critical, sarcastic, whatever, fear that. The letters reveal a lot. Or they reveal nothing, or create a totally false impression. But all these "readings" are very important and useful when meeting the individuals and working with them. It also happens that, when I meet the people face to face, I am astounded at the difference between who they are in person and how they have presented themselves in their application!

Our Letter

We send the enrolled students a letter, giving them some workshop rules. As you will see, the hours are long, with few breaks, not enough sleep hours, not enough food breaks.

WELCOME TO THE DbD EXPERIENCE!

WHEN: We will begin on Friday evening, at 6:30 pm and end at Midnight; Saturday and Sunday, we begin at 10 am and end at Midnight.

It is vital that you be ON TIME every session. PLEASE COME EARLY ON THE FIRST NIGHT to handle the details of registration. If you can, arrive by 6:00, no later than 6:15 pm.

WHERE: 2847 South Robertson Blvd, Los Angeles, CA 90034, located two doors south of Hargis Street on the west side of Robertson.

PARKING: Side streets of Robertson (Hargis or Cattaraugus), or on Robertson.

WHAT TO BRING:

1. Wear clean work clothes each day of the workshop. Comfortable, loose-fitting clothing that does not restrict movement, such as sweat pants and T-shirts, are best. Bring extra sweaters in case it gets cold at night—think layers!
2. A notepad and pen (if you want to take notes) and/or tape recorder.
3. Bottled water.

PLEASE EAT DINNER BEFORE CLASS as there is NO food break on Friday. Saturday and Sunday, there will be a 45-minute lunch break at mid-day, and a snack break in the evening. Bring some high protein snacks.

RACHEL'S RULES

By signing up for the Workshop, you agree to conform to the following:

1. At least 24 hours before the weekend, and during the sessions, NO non-prescription drugs or alcohol!
2. NO smoking anywhere on the property! Alley's OK if you do it VERY far from the building, but the Dogs will treat you with disdain.
3. There are many "Pee-Breaks" during the workshop. Try not to leave the studio during the work, unless you need to ASAP!
4. The Office equipment is off limits. No phone/computer use. Please do not move anything on the desks or put food or drinks on desks or tables where there is equipment. If you have trash at the end of the evening, please put it in the bin in the alley, NOT in the studio, so as not to attract critters.
5. Shut your cell phones off and only use them during breaks.

NOTE: Dog energy is empowering and soothing. Three dogs live in the ESPACE DbD building, and they are welcome to participate in the classes. They understand theater etiquette, and only rarely choose to perform with us. Whenever they do, however, they challenge our concentration, and if we are improvising, force us to deal with the circumstance. All well and good. But if you are allergic, please consider that we are not able to get rid of every dog hair!

Welcome one and all!

Rachel

Sasha (White Shepherd/Wolf mix) during workshop. Photo by Helena Ruffin

Friday: "Origins"

The three sessions have names: Friday is "Origins", Saturday is "Connections", and Sunday is "Power". Each day resonates with these themes, but they all bleed into one another over the weekend as a whole. All three are indispensable to the work, but I use them as titles to give a better organization to the weekend in people's minds.

Opening Circle

Rachel in circle. Photo by Helena Ruffin

The entry into the Friday session is very important and determines much of what comes later. People have to arrive earlier to register. They come through the exasperating Los Angeles traffic, often straight from their jobs. They are tense. Their anticipation of the workshop heightens their adrenalin, which is already geared to the fast life of the city and of most people's lives. The wait for the start of the workshop is usually nerve-wracking to those who are already prone to nerves. I try to greet people with enthusiasm and joy. I hug most of them, introduce the dogs, and banter and laugh. In addition to my rhythm and attitude, the way we start is key. We start in a circle, sitting on cushions or pads on the floor, and I ask the students to introduce themselves one by one, telling the group their name, and whatever they wish, briefly, about themselves and their expectation for the weekend. I begin to get a sense of personalities in that way, as do most participants, I imagine. A lot of people speak softly and mumble. Being hard of hearing, I ask them to start projecting, something I usually need to repeat throughout the days. When all the people have introduced themselves, I ask them if there are any physical ailments or limitations we should be aware of. Over the years I have taught some severely disabled people, a few in wheelchairs.

Slaves of Love

Next I introduce the two "Slaves of Love", as I call them! They are two volunteers who have already taken at least one, and usually several, DbDs. Sometimes a person who has only done one DbD becomes a Slave of Love, having volunteered because they wished to experience the workshop from another viewpoint. Both doing the DbD and seeing it from the Slave of Love vantage point teach one a great deal. They are there to help, support, make things safe and smooth, listen to gripes and deal with other problems, pass the box of paper tissues, and anything else needed, clean and make neat before and after, prepare coffee. The Slaves of Love are indispensable and carefully chosen. They can create an atmosphere that is anxious or easy. They can have a lot of influence on the way a DbD goes. These people must be able to melt into the background while oiling all the gears! They are also of great importance in their help to me, shielding me from trivial problems, and giving me energy if I seem to be flagging. It is important for me to manage my energy for the long hours, every minute of which I am alert and working, and fully focused. I also don't want to be distracted by things that don't pertain to the workshop. The Slaves take the bullet for me. Love them! We sometimes discuss specific people, their work or their problems, or talk about the parts of the work that have been beautiful and successful.

After the intros, I give the initial talk, as I do every day, starting by laying out several additional rules.

Rules

The main rule is: "Do not use physical force". It is clumsy, sloppy, dangerous, and not theatrical. All strong emotions such as violence, anger, possessiveness, can be expressed with what I call "Power at a Distance". I give the example of classical Asian theater where duels are fought, people wrestle; wars are waged, all at a distance, without touching, and giving fully the impression of danger and homicidal fury. Another rule is that if a prop or costume is broken or damaged, it must be repaired or replaced, or an equivalent object must be turned in.

I also ask the players not to leave the room—there are enough breaks—and not to stretch out on the beckoning cushions and pads. Always keep their spines straight and high or the energy of the room begins to sag.

A very important rule is what I call "Taking the Hat"! Taking the hat or any article of clothing, prop, or mask from another performer is usually forbidden. It occurs when a player is on stage but doesn't know what his persona is, why he or she is there, what to do with themselves. So, for want of something better to do, they take another player's hat! The costume is a second skin. Abusing it and/or grabbing it is akin to flaying the character. To needlessly or meaninglessly steal any part of it is almost always discernable to an audience as a major boo-boo.

Note: In the event of this occurrence, and to somehow save the day, that action must be made to become the *main plot*. It must be played, made important and meaningful, become a focal point and given power. There is nothing worse than a bunch of discarded objects dropped on the stage floor, pitifully lying there and trampled, without having added anything to the stage event.

The space we work in is a white box, with real theatrical lights this time, not the old clamp-on lights of Instant Theatre—although we do have them and use them when needed—a light board, several sound boxes, a music and sound instrument table on wheels, an adjacent room filled to the brim with objects, hats, masks, fabric, and costumes or parts of costumes of all kinds, all stuff collected over decades, some inherently precious, some having become precious through use and association.

Masks. Photo by Kate Noonan

Props. Photo by Kate Noonan

Many of these things are donations, gifts that are seldom announced and that appear during the performances as pleasant surprises. Set pieces line some walls, all painted white. There are three flats, two black and one white, on wheels, that can be easily moved. The lights are gelled in saturated colors, and the white sets them off. There is a sense of magic in these rooms and in the things that inhabit them. These premises should not be approached otherwise than with respect, and a sense of the sacred. Sacred is as sacred does. A place can be easily desecrated by bringing to it bad humor, strife, the problems of the life outside, chit-chat, gossip, or chewing gum! When you come to this place, you leave all that behind. It is no religious shrine, but it is the place where you mine and bring to light the best that you are and are capable of. Art-making is very difficult. It is a demanding mistress. If not approached with that understanding, if made trivial and banal, it won't yield its secrets and possibilities. But bring your devotion and humility, your patience and understanding, your determination to create and create well, and the space and everything in it will provide and support.

Just Do It!

All DbD activities are to be executed at full throttle, not indicated as in some rehearsal practices, but making full-fledged art pieces at every opportunity, and not sloughing over the assignment, reverting to old habits and mannerisms. Often people don't do that because they are afraid of "blowing their wad" and dispersing their energy and inventiveness "before the fact". It never happens that way. There is no "Before the Fact", because every move is a "Fact"! Every opportunity for creativity should be used fully with no holding back. No "indicating", please! Just DO IT!

The Genie

When magical things happen in the performance space, we say, "The Genie is here!" And it is palpable. Amazing things happen: coincidences, synchronicities, realizations, esthetic heights, spontaneous finds. It's the Genie of the place responding to being honored, manifesting through the art work, and it's like nothing else. It is sheer ecstasy!

"The Genie", perhaps! Photographer unknown

Circle Talk: "Origins"

All my talks are improvised and contain material and thoughts that are prominent in my life at the time of the particular DbD. I also don't always follow the curriculum or the order of processes as laid out here. So much depends on the energy of the group, my intuition as to what to say and what to do, and any other event that may pull in one direction or another. But the basic content is as follows.

> Memory and imagination are the locomotives of art, and especially of the art of theatrical improvisation. Memory goes back a long way, and helped by knowledge and whatever erudition we possess, imagination moves in to fill in and animate what we already know of our past. We know some things

connecting us to a family, an extended family, a clan, a tribe. What we don't know we can guess. Going back further, we can imagine a life, a society we never experienced first hand. If our origins were European, we may or not be aware of when we came to the United States, and under what conditions. If we came here from other continents, were we forced, were we compelled by politics, were we curious and hopeful? We can imagine the land of America as it was then, our relationship to people of different color and social status. We can see what wildlife existed then. So we fill in the gaps. Going further back, we may change continents, and dip into the history of our ancient place of origin. If we came from South or Central America, from Africa or from Asia, we must learn the history of, and about life under, their great civilizations. If we came from Europe, there is a rich and sometimes frightening history. Perhaps life in a shtetl, if one is Jewish, pogroms, deportation, persecution, genocide. If Christian, religious wars, Inquisition, crusades, and the gradual establishment of a moral code; life "brutish and short", or, if members of the landed aristocracy or royalty, wielding absolute power, constantly fighting to hold on to it. Further back, the great Mediterranean civilizations, the Barbarian invasions; further back still, centuries of empire building, of religious diversity, and the slow and inexorable domestication of the wild. We can project ourselves in Neolithic and before that, Paleolithic times. The struggle to make the Earth yield its treasures in an accessible way, the birth and growth of agriculture and husbandry, and the enmity between the two; the advent of culture and art. Further back still, we live in deserts, in forests, near water. We gather plants, kill prey, eat and wear it, focus on survival and avoiding being eaten. We develop language and communicate in bands that create a certain social order, different for different bands. We develop language. We are mostly nomadic, and our line will eventually descend on the sedentary, to replace and eradicate them. But we become sedentary ourselves and defend our turf. I can even imagine the years, centuries and millennia of amazing transformations of the Earth, its inhabitants, and its appearance. Continents glide on their tectonic plates, stretching and tightening oceans, lifting mountains. Animals are huge, climate changes and extinctions abound. Wind and rain soften the continents' profiles. Before that, billions of years go by with oceans teeming with tiny unchanging organisms slowly developing themselves and their survival strategies, blooming suddenly into myriads of forms that will engender a number of animals that remain to transform themselves, explore their world, and colonize it. Before that, there is the planet slowly and cataclysmically striving to become a viable orbiting satellite of our star the Sun, its crust suffering the constant blows of asteroids from space, absorbing the water and gases that they unleash as they make contact, transforming Earth into the water planet, rendering it fertile, able to sculpt its own surface and redesign its atmosphere, taking the bite out of oxygen to make it sustain life. But our imagination doesn't stop there. The planet Earth needs to ignite itself at its core, give birth to our one satellite the Moon, spew fire and metal from its depth and renew itself constantly, in motion around our star, slowly achieving an even temperature and atmosphere capable of birthing and nurturing life. There is a Cosmos, a Universe out there, perhaps many, invisible to us. There are infinite mysteries still to be fathomed. The miracle of our reality, our life, our formation, our history and histories, and finally our present time with its complications, its beauties, its horrors, are all material that we draw from in our theatrical compositions. There is no end to the possibilities at our disposal. Our origins feed our creativity and us. We are made of these origins. Our bodies are air, water, minerals, live cells; our brains replicate all of evolution, and our minds contain all the collective unconscious we need to use these things in movement, sound, content and meaning, in our work. All we require is to listen, to learn, to allow our minds to reach into those deep folds and our bodies to respond with motion and sound, in order to attain these far-away, alien and long-forgotten states. Thus do we discover what we are made of, what we can portray, what we can become, for the short episodes of theatrical improvisations, in ways surprising, unexpected, and thoroughly satisfying, for they correspond to realities dormant in our global unconscious, but at the ready when called forth.

TECHNIQUES

The Triangle and No-Focus Focus

I then describe two very important and fundamental ideas or techniques about the work we do:

1 I present a triangle that I create with my hands and fingers, and say: "Our work is a Triangle": the first angle is you, "the Performer". The second angle is what I call "the Partnership", which is everything else on stage with you: space, other players, objects, set, lights, sound, air, gravity, noise, etc. All these things are of equal importance, and the Performer's way of involving them, and interacting with them, is what creates the Stage Event. The third angle is "the Audience". I am very aware and respectful of the Audience, and believe that no piece is quite done until an audience has experienced it. Theater is based

on that collaboration. An audience (always different in volume, mood, expectation, and understanding) will put the final touches on the stage event, by their reaction. It will tell you what's funny and what's not. Not in words, but in whatever energy it sends back to you when you are performing. It will let you know if it needs to laugh or cry, and when it's bored. It will establish a rhythm. You can then emphasize your playing in that direction or attempt to transform an audience as you perform. Playing to an audience is like the final action performed by the old sword smiths, to "baptize" their finished swords, by making them taste fresh blood . . .

2 The second technique I call "No-Focus Focus". As they sit in the circle I ask the students to focus their vision on the face of the person across from them, and to really see that face in every detail. I ask them to notice how peripheral vision disappears the more precise the view of the face. Now, imagine that a string is tied between the viewer's nose and the nose of the viewed, and slowly move your eye focus across that imaginary line, until you are focusing on the air before your own nose, as close to your face as you can without discomfort. Slide your vision across and back along that imaginary string, and stop where you are comfortable. You no longer see the face on the opposite side of the circle clearly and accurately, but your peripheral vision has opened up and you now take in a far larger space, albeit fuzzy, without having to turn toward what you wish to see. I tell the students to then focus through the face and through the opposite wall, on the horizon they imagine seeing. That too is No-Focus Focus. This technique is important for several reasons: it allows you to "see" what is happening on stage without having to move your head and focus your eyes, which often destroys the effect you are trying to create; it allows you to seem to make eye contact with members of the audience while not actually seeing them (which may be distracting); and it can also put you in a slight trance, which can be beneficial in our work. In any case, it creates an invisible "bubble" around you and can allow you to focus on the inner wall of that bubble. If you do that, you can also move your head with your eyes focused front, the eyeball not moving from the middle of the socket, and the gaze perpendicular to your face. This gives the performer a "non-human" look, useful for portraying animals, ghosts, intangibles, sculptures, weather, plants, etc. It's an important technique because the expression and visibility of eyes on stage clearly indicate a thinking human and gives us away if we are trying to personify a non-human.

When the Friday opening circle is ended, I have the group stand facing me, in any formation they wish, so long as they have a certain amount of space around them.

Guided Standing and Moving Meditation

Stand tall, legs slightly apart, feet parallel, arms at your side, relaxed, and in No-Focus Focus. Don't *do* anything. Listen to the silence. Every space has its own kind of silence.

Now pay attention to the space, taking it in without moving. Where are you, what is the feel of this volume of air? Be aware of breathing in the space, and of sharing your breath with other sentient and live beings. Be aware of the column of air that rests on your shoulders, and the sea of air in which you live. It's our atmosphere, made up meticulously of certain gases in a specific amount, that keep you alive, and also allow you to move, grow and develop in a way peculiar to the inhabitants of this planet. You would not be able to move the way you do if you were on the Moon, or on Mars, for instance. Touch your air and slowly move your hands and arms as if you lived in an ocean. You do. It's an ocean of air.

Now stand still again, and be aware of the Earth under your feet. It has something we call gravity that pulls us toward its center. Our walking erect, as bipeds, unlike most other creatures on our planet, is a continual balancing act that is tiring and even dangerous to our spine, but that we rarely notice anymore, except as babies attempting to walk erect and falling. Walking is falling and catching ourselves with our legs and feet. Unconsciously we keep adjusting our center of gravity. Move your body very slightly until you feel you will fall, and adjust. That way you sense a "safe" sphere in which to operate.

Put your attention on your feet, and imagine digging them and yourself through this floor and into the Earth, deep into the crust, deeper through the tectonic plate; below that, down into the viscous mantle, spiraling down with the convection currents into the outer core; deeper into the center of the planet, where the heart of her Power lies.

Take some of that Power. Fill up with it! There's plenty more where that came from! But ask first, and say thank you after taking your fill!

Return, retracing your itinerary: out of the core, up the convection currents of the mantle, through the tectonic plate, up into the crust, through the floor and back in the studio. When you learn to fill yourself with Power and begin to radiate it, this is what people call "stage presence", a very real emanation of individual Power that can have a huge effect on an audience.

A slow, meditative music begins to play. (The music is usually Annea Lockwood's *Thousand Year Dreaming* CD. Occasionally it is John Cage's *Music for Piano and Prepared Piano*, or a Ki/Kitaro Japanese CD.)

> Earth Power is your birthright, as is that of everything in Nature. Feel, within your body, where this Power or energy seems to pool, to be most dense, and begin moving from that place. It can be neck, fingers, eyes, abdomen, toes . . . wherever the heat is, wishing to explode. Let it motor that part of the body which, in turn, will set adjacent parts in motion, then moving more parts, until the entire body moves, saturated with Earth Power.

As I speak over the music, people begin to move. They explore not only their own bodies and locomotion, but also their place and position in the space, how that affects them, and how far they can go in this exploration. I watch and notice how people approach the exercise, if they are reticent and self-conscious, if they avoid touching others, if they watch around them to compare what others are doing with what they are doing, etc., or if they are fully there, aware of their surroundings but centered, and enjoying the surprises of the moment. A lot can be learned in this initial exercise.

After a while, I give different suggestions:

> Be aware of your impulses and those of others. Feel it when you approach another student, when you enter a different orbit, or field. Get a sense of your reaction to being close to a body: is it inviting, recoiling, on show? What waves do you emanate?

A "freeze" during a movement meditation. Photo by Helena Ruffin

Sometimes, I call "Freeze!" and have people stop in their tracks, feeling their frozen impulse interrupted, and becoming aware of the "constellation" formed by the bodies in a one-time-only configuration, never to be repeated, as well as their own frozen motion: where was it going? What was it trying to say? Sometimes I have the group run in all directions as fast as possible, without collisions. Or to go into slow motion as if they were wading in glycerin. At times, in a freeze or a pile-up, I ask people to emit a sound, which can build into more sounds, and peak as a chant or chorale. The piece ends as the students "melt" to the floor. The Slave of Love fades the lights to blackout.

"Seed to Tree" is an exercise sometimes given in various versions in acting classes. The players begin on the floor, as a seed that I describe as "the most minimal space that envelops the greatest potential." I have them decide in their own minds what plant they will grow into. There is music played during this exercise, by Toru Takemitsu. The seeds break ground, grow, absorb the sunlight that they transform into food, flower, then make fruit, go to seed, and wilt and die. When dead, they become food for other organisms, and thus life continues cyclically. The exercise differs from those in other classes that I'm aware of, inasmuch as it goes beyond death, making it a nurturing part of the life cycle.

Seed to Tree

Exercises such as this one are all designed to take people beyond the "me" stage, and to begin to discover in themselves the life and biology of non-humans. This exploration is vital for breaking stylistic habits and human mannerisms. I ask those who are good dancers to refrain from "dancing". They are to move from another source, and not worry about "expressive" dancing or the need to "look good". That "looking good" business is the hardest habit to break. To me, "good" is not how skillfully you do something you were taught, but rather discovering something within you that

"Seed to Tree". Photo by Kate Noonan

is "like" what you are portraying, but in a way that is totally new, unexpected, surprising, and satisfyingly right. Every student turns up a different plant; a tree, a clinging vine held up by the studio wall, etc. They instinctively realize what goes into the growth and development of vegetation, and what role Time plays in its life. All have to find in themselves the life force that is not centralized in specialized organs, but disseminated throughout the whole plant, with few "specializations", such as the buds or the roots. This forces them to move in ways that are unfamiliar and that engender new performing styles. Some plants are carnivores, others develop ways of protecting themselves against herbivores or parasites, and many (who don't depend on the wind) must invent strategies for attracting insects or birds who will be their sexual ambassadors to scatter their progeny far and wide. It's a constant fight to live and propagate, and there is very little of the romantic prettiness that people usually associate with plants. The effort involved in losing the human experience while attempting to embody a vegetable life brings new discoveries and realizations. It brings "origins" into focus.

Note: Beware T-shirt adjustment or hair pulling! This is telltale evidence that the student is not focused on the art work but, again, on "looking good"! Also, either closed eyes or No-Focus Focus is needed in the above process.

PAIRED-OFF PROCESSES

These are exercises that form the basis for some of the most important components of the style I teach. The first two, "Ball of Fire" and "Mirrors", are the scaffolding for "Units"; the others, "Dolls" and "Dolls at a Distance", prepare for "Power at a Distance Dance".

Ball of Fire

After the students are randomly paired-off, I position them facing each other, two feet apart, standing relaxed, *doing nothing but looking at one another.* This is very hard on some people, since staring is taboo in our society. I ask them to *see* the other person as if they were an unknown object, seen for the first time, and not a person at all. At this point, people become uneasy, and it expresses itself in smiles and

"Ball of Fire". Photo by Kate Noonan

sometimes giggles. I put a stop to that, saying, "Don't do anything but look. Don't be 'charming'. Don't try to seduce your partner!" That brings one last chuckle and then there is focus on the exercise. I physically touch those faces whose muscles tense into a habitual grin. This starter continues to separate people from their social personae, and cleanses them of learned attitudes.

So far, there is no music, neither is there any in the following process. I ask the students, still standing with relaxed arms, facing and gazing at the partner, to fill themselves with Power. To radiate it out to the person they face, without moving or changing expression. Both do that at the same time, so they must be able to emit and receive simultaneously, an In-and-Out exercise. After a few seconds, they go back to neutral. Zero. I have them repeat the exercise and perform it three times, raising the intensity by more and more decibels each time. Finally, they rotate their hanging arms so that the palms of their hands face each other. I have them focus their attention on both the faces and the palms of their hands, noticing the very real exchange of energy that passes like bolts of lightning between the palms. When they are physically aware of this shared energy, they visualize it as a fiery mass, held by four hands. They mold and sculpt it between them, forcing it into a dense ball of fire, or stretching it into a large and less dense object that I call "fire taffy". They move, carrying the ball and sustaining it between them, walking forward toward each other or backwards and away. They minimize the space between them when they feel they are losing the sensation of the fiery ball, augmenting the distance when they are confident it is still there. Finally, I have them make the ball smaller and smaller, denser and denser, until it is the size of a football, then a tennis ball, and a golf ball. I then have them push through the ball and touch hands, thus recreating the fire ball in their two bodies, coming together, touching and hugging, and sharing their combined energies in an embrace.

The whole process promotes non-verbal intimacy and communication. It is important, at the outset of the workshop, to eradicate as much as possible the gender attitudes we always carry with us in this society. I also want to go beyond personality, and into energies. After a few seconds, I ask them to "go back to neutral, relax and breathe, and acknowledge the partner". At which point there are usually a few seconds of giggles. I say "Change partners!" and they do, also randomly.

During the Mirrors and Dolls exercises, I give instructions as needed. I also walk among the players and administer quick individual corrections. I do this in group exercises but not in the pieces that are presented to the students and myself as audience. In that circumstance, I sit and watch all the way through, as do the rest of the spectators, and give feedback when it's over. There is always applause, whether the work is deemed good or not, to underline the fact that the exercise is completed. A good piece is enthusiastically applauded, and also whooped!

Mirrors

"Mirrors" are the exercises that prepare for "Units", which I will describe later. They deal with unison, and the ability to create it improvisationally. It is a fundamental technique that must be mastered early on, as most choreography, blocking or direction utilizes what I call Unit work.

I put on a CD at this point. I like John Cage's early short works on prepared piano. Still paired, I ask the students to mirror each other's movements. But instead of having a mirror and a person, I tell them that there is no leader, that they must do unison in "floating leadership", and alternate subtly between them as to who leads and who follows. After a while, when the players begin to sense the partner's rhythm, his or her resistance or availability, both begin to "mirror" almost instantaneously, anticipating each other's moves. They become as one. But it is mandatory that they sense the other person's style, the speed with which they react, the capabilities of their bodies. No-Focus Focus is needed here, as it opens peripheral vision of the whole body in front of you, and shows where the weight is transferred, thus anticipating the next move. Empathy is needed, and a willingness to be equal rather than ahead of the other. A strong lesson is learned, without emphasizing it verbally, and a technique established that will be of great importance in the improvisation work.

Shadows

When most pairs succeed in face-to-face mirroring, I have them learn "shadowing". One person is behind the other, and has to copy the leader as seen from behind. As people move through the space, those in front or in back shift, with the shadows automatically becoming leaders and the leaders becoming shadows, while continuing the unison seamlessly.

Puppets

When Shadows is mastered, I ask the person who is behind to shadow, but as if they are causing the front person to move. In reality, the person in the back is the one copying the motion of the front person, but seeming to be like a puppeteer or wizard causing the front person's motions.

Dolls

This exercise is also fundamental to our style. There is a "sculptor" and a "doll", which is that little wooden effigy with ball-bearing articulations, used by sculptors in the past. Again, after people "relax and breathe, acknowledge the partner and change partners", I ask them to decide who is the sculptor and who is the sculptor's "doll". I demonstrate with a Slave of Love. The "sculptor" moves the "doll" physically, one articulation at a time, to create the gestures and attitudes of the sculptor's imagination. The latter must learn where the center of gravity is so as not to topple the doll. The exercise is about learning about the human body and its motor and expressive capabilities, and the doll is often placed in gestures they would not ordinarily execute on their own. It also shows where equilibrium rests, and forces attention on body memory. The doll must stay in whatever position it is placed for as long as the sculptor doesn't change it. The sculptor must immobilize the part that is attached to the articulation he/she is moving, so as to only activate one articulation at a time, and not drag another with it. For instance, if only the forearm is to move, the upper arm must be immobilized by one of the sculptor's hands, while the other hand places the forearm wherever he or she wishes it to be. After a while, many attitudes have been imposed on the "dolls", and I have people "freeze" and exchange roles.

Dolls at a Distance

"Dolls at a Distance" is a difficult process, and one that takes longer to master. It is the culmination of the Mirrors and Dolls exercises. "Dolls" is preparation for "Dolls at a Distance" which, in turn, is preparation for "Power at a Distance Dance", a very important technique. Again, people "breathe, acknowledge the partner and change partners". By this time, people have experienced working with many different partners in a way that teaches them how various bodies move, how reticent or willing the bodies of partners are to respond, and what kind of person they are, in a general way. This knowledge tells people what to expect and how to deal with different kinds of personalities. "Dolls at a Distance" repeats the "Dolls" exercise, but "at a distance". The partners stand about six feet from one another. The sculptor begins to manipulate the doll, using the same moves as before, but "at a distance", actually manipulating air. Funny how hard that is to do! People often have no sense of distance, volume, level, or how the hands grab, pull, contain, push, etc., and what articulation to activate and which one to block, in order to achieve the pose they are aiming for. The exercise should increase body awareness and memory. I often

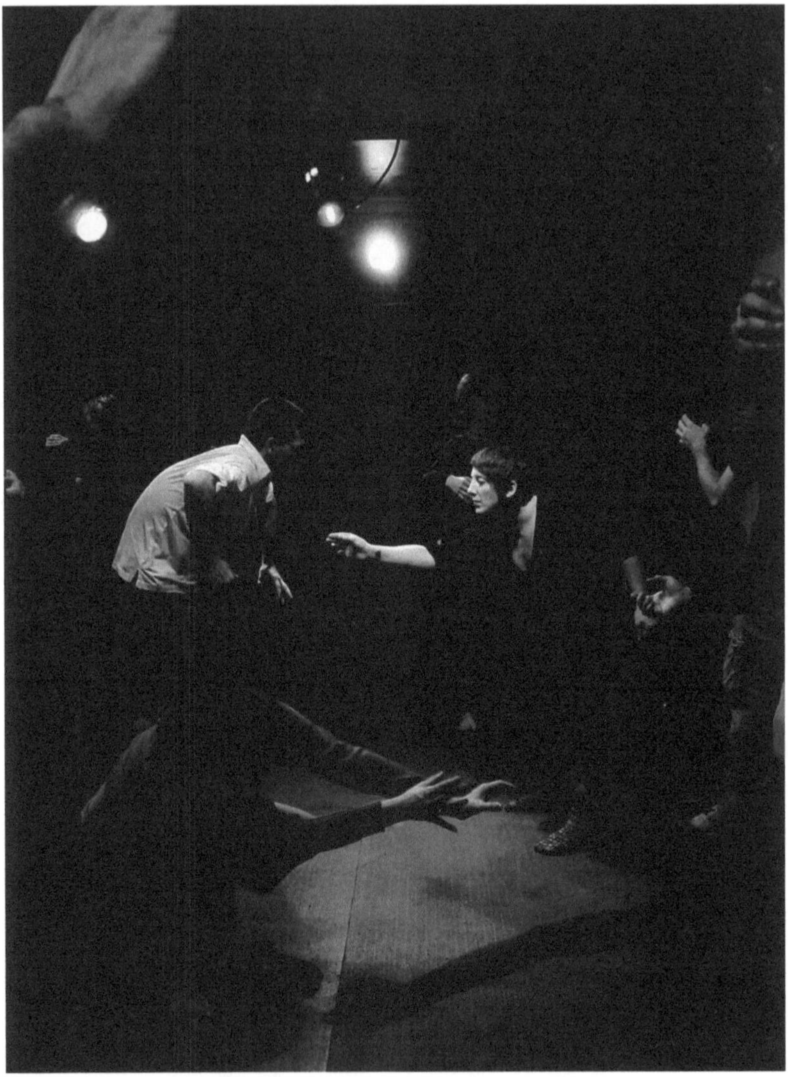

"Dolls at a Distance". Photo by Kate Noonan

have people cross the six-foot distance and touch and move the doll as in the "Dolls" exercise, then go back and do the same thing at a distance. In a way it's a mime problem, but it's more than that. It's about communication, empathy, and knowledge of the human body. When the moves are right, i.e. imitate correctly the gestures needed to move parts of a body, the "dolls" can decipher what is wanted of them and respond with the corresponding move. If they can't understand the sculptor's actions, they cannot move, and the sculptor must readjust his/her hands in order to make his gestures readable. This underlines the need for clarity in the sculptor, and availability in the doll. The sculptors must also be careful not to "indicate", "direct", "order" or "mirror". In other words, in no way "do" the gestures themselves, a tempting action when the doll doesn't respond in the desired way. It is also important for the two partners to feel each other's velocity of response. The sculptor must not move faster than the doll, as he or she is supposed to be actually moving a body part and must sustain the illusion of so doing, even at a distance. Additionally, the doll must not second-guess the sculptor's wishes and run ahead of the motions that will ostensibly activate their wooden frame. During this exercise I must check everyone all the time, interfere and demonstrate individually. It's not an easy exercise, it is done with enormous effort and concentration, and people come out of it sometimes as if out of a slight trance.

Power at a Distance Dance

Change of music to something dramatic. New partners. This is a movement exercise based on "Dolls at a Distance", where, throughout the dance, the choreography consists of action and reaction, cause and effect. People in their pairs take turns in positive and negative movement, the positive being dominant, the negative being the recipient of those moves, immediately becoming dominant in return.

Example: Player A mimes throwing, player B mimes being hit. B retaliates in a pushing movement, and A falls. A gets up and mimes a slap in the face. B staggers. B blows a kiss. A mimes catching it. Etc. All at a distance. A seesaw action, or a pendulum. Now me, now you. When this realistic section is done, there should be real dance choreography, improvised on the theme of action and reaction, but using abstract movement and depending more on dynamics than on recognizable actions.

Power at a Distance in Improvisation

In the initial work involving Power at a Distance, the stage must be readable to everyone at all times. To achieve that, No-Focus Focus must be used. The front player in a group may initiate moves in response to someone doing Power at a Distance, and so must shadow the responder. The Power may, for instance, be a pull. The front person of your group responds by being pulled, and you, as shadow must also be pulled. The "Shadow" behind you must then follow your lead and then all are being pulled. If the action is in a place that makes you the front person, your responsibility is to respond and lead the others. You remember the admonition *be where you're needed.* You also must *do as needed.* Or find a way of getting out of it that introduces a new direction in the Stage Event. Whatever you do, don't drop the ball. If someone begins a Power at a Distance move and it is not received or noticed, the hole it creates in the piece is palpable and embarrassing. It tears the continuity, and rebounds badly for the players involved. What makes it worse is that the tendency then is for the aggressor to substitute moves that involve bodily contact, pushing, pulling or other messy and forbidden actions. If that happens, it is usually very gauche. However, bodily contact is not a taboo. It can happen in a way that nourishes the theme of the piece without getting messy.

After the Paired-Off Processes, there is usually one of our breaks (a small one, for a quick snack and bathroom needs). When the students return, there is a period of attention to the visual aspect of the work.

DEMONSTRATIONS

The students take their places as audience, against the wall, sitting on pads and cushions on the floor. I ask for two volunteers to make a simple set, using our set pieces and possibly a prop and a *shmatte* (Yiddish for fabric, or rag). We have several lengths of fabric of different colors and textures, to dress the sets and use as props or pieces of costumes. We call them all *shmattes*. The two set-makers work collaboratively, sometimes with one person being the main designer and the other a helper, usually needed to carry platforms or wooden boxes and pedestals. When the set is done, usually in about two minutes, they sit down, and I critique it. Often, the set looks like window dressing: something nice in the center, with no room for playing areas except those surrounding the centerpiece. Or perhaps the set pieces will be equidistant from one another, making a dull set with no dynamics in the space. I suggest that every set made must create a completely new and unexpected use of the space, making the room unrecognizable. People then stretch their imagination, putting more demands on themselves to concoct something exciting out of a seemingly simple and stale assignment. They realize that our bland, white screens, ladders, simple flats on wheels, and boxes, may become magical if well placed and well lit. They can also tell a "story".

Set demonstrations. Photo by Helena Ruffin

Performers in set. Photographer unknown

After I show the difference between a so-so set and an exciting one, I get on the light board and light it. Or a Slave of Love lights it. Few lights are turned on, because if too many lamps are lit, we get a boring general lighting. General lighting doesn't emphasize how one is to read the set, either for the content of the story, or for the emotional atmosphere and important focus in the moment of drama, or for its style. Sometimes as few as one, two, or three lights, sensitively calibrated, can express a strong statement of meaning and emotion, that too many lights would confuse or erase. I ask the students to tell me the "story" as told by the set and the lights, and they do. I then change to at least two other light designs, and have them read the "story" of those also. I illustrate the importance of lighting in a piece, and the responsibility of the lighting person who improvises with the players. The light must not only facilitate seeing the important sections of the piece, but also give the mood, sometimes changing it when there is a feeling of the piece going nowhere, and also putting focus and emphasis where it's needed while de-emphasizing those areas that are dormant or uninteresting. As we all know, lighting is immensely important, a prime art form in its own right, and lighting designers such as Robert Wilson are seen as great artists. Theatrical lighting has developed immensely, with the advent of electricity in the late nineteenth and beginning twentieth centuries. It then began to be used for mood and emotional effects, no longer simply "to light the action". In the second half of the twentieth century, through rock concerts, musicals, and dance, lighting became an art. It can make or break a piece, and a great deal of attention is placed on it in my workshops.

After we "tell the story" with just set and lights, I ask a volunteer to go into the set with its lighting, and strike a pose in a place of her or his choosing and freeze. Sometimes the student does something very dramatic, sometimes more matter-of-fact. I then ask the "audience" to volunteer a new "story" that explains the image we see before us. Several people respond. I don't contradict or critique these responses because they all belong to and illuminate the speaker, showing us where his imagination takes him. It becomes obvious to people that response to a theatrical offering is truly an individual and unique process, and that pieces may be read in many different ways. I then ask the person in the set to change their position, as we change the lights. I repeat the request for more interpretations. I then add another player to take their place in the set, taking the first player into consideration. The two then present a new readable "story". The audience interprets it again. These demonstrations can go on for 15 to 30 minutes, as needed, with as many people volunteering to be in the set, as many light changes, as many set changes as I deem necessary to teach whatever lesson is inherent and called for in the demonstration.

FORMS

Units

In the Friday session I teach several fundamental exercises which establish the basis for the form and style of my theatrical work. When Friday is over, the students come to the rest of the weekend with enough basic techniques and skills, as well as a common vocabulary, to be able to achieve excellent theatrical pieces, both structured and freely improvised, as solos or ensemble. New and varied techniques are learned subsequently, but what is taught on Friday is the pillar on which all others are erected. "Units" is the "can't do without" technique of my work, one of the most important forms I teach in the DbD Experience. Simply put, it's a choreographic "must" that we see in almost every production of dance there is. A Unit, in my teaching, is two people, or more, who perform the same movements, as in "Mirrors" and "Shadows". As abstract movement, they are a dance ploy. As representing a recognizable entity, they are what I call "a story". They can be parts of the same entity, as for instance, several players portraying a tree by embodying the branches, or they can be individuals that are part of a group, as wolves in a pack. The unison can be precise or not, so long as it is recognizably similar, and the performers are close to each other. The further away from one another they are, the more precise must be the unison work, to make it clear that they form a Unit. You can see unit work in ballet, in jazz, in the Rockettes, in musicals, in world theater, in contemporary dance. You can see Units in everyday life, if you look for it: people waiting in line, people working in factories, people grouping themselves in demonstrations, in sports, in tourism, marching in armies. There are Units everywhere. On stage and in improvisation, it becomes a major technique for organizing the space. If all participants in a group piece perform as soloists throughout, the composition of the stage becomes distracting, muddled, chaotic and difficult to follow. Or you have the fashion show effect, with players as models on the runway, showing off their costumes and their individual personae. But with even a feeble attempt at forming Units, the improvisation appears structured, readable, and shaped. Units are not rigid. They may form and disband. They may appear briefly, or create variations on a theme. They can function as rhythmic counterpoint; they may meld into each other, or be small or large at will.

Out of Units solos or duets may emerge. Sometimes, a Unit formed by the whole group doing unison may break up into individual pieces. But soon enough, new Units should be formed. Without unit work, only very advanced students can remain well delineated and formally satisfying. The magic of Units is exposed in free improvisation, when the formations are spontaneous, simultaneous and symmetrical, although never discussed, choreographed, or rehearsed. Therein lies the unique and wondrous effect of free improvisation. An audience who has been told that what they see was never directed or discussed, will have trouble believing it if it is well done, and will be totally enchanted by the sudden formations, and the way the possibility of chaos and disintegration is handled and averted.

I am a stickler for *Form*. Most of my initial feedback to the students has to do with Form, Composition, Shape and Structure: the abstract scaffolding or skeleton of a piece. Sometimes, the Form *is* the piece. The story takes its intensity, its meaning, its importance from its form. Without attention to form, what you get is shagginess, and a jumble.

I especially relish seeing the effort of unison work improvised. It is rare that the moves are in instantaneous unison for it takes a split second for a visual or audio stimulus to reach the brain, and another split second for the body to respond in kind. It is that very slight "décalage" that I love, as it trembles and teeters between the mirror image and the fall into the precipice of chaos.

Levels

In DbD vocabulary, a "Level" is a stratum of being. For instance, a human is on one Level. A boulder on another. A cloud, on yet another. When a performer or a unit of performers portrays a flock of birds, and another unit portrays a blizzard, they are on different "Levels". As a result, they cannot communicate, connect, or even see each other directly as would performers playing on the same level. The abstract connection of form is there, but achieved by indirect means: by sound, movement, rhythm, etc. To mark the difference in levels, several techniques are useful: first, the eyes. Don't make eye contact with those playing on a different level. Use No-Focus Focus. If the eyes of the Unit playing the blizzard are visible (not hidden by a mask, for instance, or a *shmatte*), those eyes must not seem "human". They must remain rigidly within the socket, carried by the head and neck, but immobile within the face. Another approach is spatial: birds can move fast and use space incoherently, fluttering to and fro. Whereas the blizzard must move very slowly and cover a simple line, say from Stage Left to Stage Right or in a wide circle, in slow motion for the duration of the piece.

When one level is more menacing or frightening than the other, its power must be expressed mainly by the way the weaker level reacts to it. Fear is portrayed by the frightened, not by the fear-inducing. In films, the suspense of a scene is often expressed in the victim's behavior and expression, not by the menace itself. Stage Power must be given, not taken. Sometimes, a Powerful entity will remain motionless and blank while others will cower and tremble before it. There are endless ways of portraying different levels on stage, and discovering them can become a measure of our sensitivity and imagination.

Units and Levels

These improvisations don't need a plot; therefore the players don't have to search for the "story". What these exercises look to achieve is good set-making showing a sense of playing areas, visual stimulation, originality, and a good understanding and use of Units and Levels. They are short pieces with multi-casts, and need to display how to use the stage without crowding, with a sense of form and spatial relationship. Most of all, they show how to work in Units with good unison and awareness, as well as the imagination for evoking non-human as well as human entities and how they relate to each other. Levels must be understood thus, and quickly analyzed: are there two different levels? More? Is there only one? The way the players personify different levels contributes to the magic of the improvised piece. Levels make ample use of "Puppets", "Power at a Distance Dance", "No-Focus Focus", and "Unit" work. The way different levels are presented gives space and breadth to the stage, making clear that very different entities are involved in the same piece. "Puppets", for instance, may be used by a four-Unit "Blizzard" on the platform, upstage of the "Crows", thus illustrating their power and effect on the birds while never being obviously aware of them.

These "rules" of mine are used because they advance the work by leapfrogging over the most habitual hurdles, thus allowing great jumps in skill and knowledge, and as a result, help people attain the goal of wonderful theater in record time. The "rules" are not to be taken as taboos. All rules can be broken, so long as they have been understood, used, and mastered. If they are ignored or contradicted, it must be for a good reason, and done with skill. The DbD is not designed for advanced performers, although some of the participants are advanced performers in their own right, or people who have taken my workshops in the past. The Rules and Processes establish a grammar that all learn at the same time, along with the vocabulary they use as the weekend progresses. The depth of understanding with which theater is eventually invented and performed is experienced as the result of the strong base on which the technique is built and the seriousness and dedication with which it is learned.

FEEDBACK

When a piece is over, after the ending blackout and the return of the lights, I ask the students to remain on stage to get feedback. I discourage the players' participation in the discussion. The purpose of feedback is for the performers to hear what it is that was received by an audience, and to learn to what extent what was intended was experienced and perceived by the individual spectator. The players also realize how divergent the interpretations of an audience might be. They don't need to answer or explain what they did and why they did it. Both groups, the performers and the spectators, are learning what they need to learn, without discussion. I sometimes tell the players: "Don't tell me how *you* feel! Find out how *we* (the spectators) feel!"

I begin by giving feedback myself to set the tone for the rest of the "audience" to give their feedback, and show by example how to critique without humiliating the player. Always give positive feedback, and show how missteps can be avoided and how the next opportunity can be met. Only in workshop do the players have the chance to find out if their intentions were communicated or not. Art making is never finished. You don't ever reach a point of total satisfaction or perfection. But when a person shows progress, it must be acknowledged, nurtured, and applauded. People are trained like dogs—by the positive reinforcement method! (It should be understood here that my comparing people to dogs is a compliment in my view!)

GROUP IMPROVISATIONS

In the time that is left on Friday night, we do two types of group improvisations: one with a theme, one without. The first one is done twice, with two groups of equal amounts of people, so as to have an audience and not crowd the stage. The second features the entire class and is a free improvisation that may use all that was learned so far, and adapt those techniques to whatever the moment brings. If the group number is twelve, six people will perform each of the themed pieces. The free piece at the end will comprise all twelve.

With theme: "The Mayan Temple and the Jungle"

The music for this piece is the beginning of Stravinsky's *Rite of Spring*. The set is simply two eight-feet long by three-feet wide platforms side by side, forming an eight-feet by six-feet surface, the long side parallel to the audience. If there are six people performing, I will ask for a Unit of Four and a Unit of Two. The Unit of Four will portray a Jungle, and the Unit of Two will be a Mayan Temple. The "story" is as follows:

> A rich town during the reign of the Mayas is building a temple in a sacred space. The encroaching jungle is pushed back with machetes by the people and not allowed to invade the square where the temple rises. When the temple is built, it enjoys several years of power and glory, being the center of the town's cultural and religious life and the place of ritual and sacrifice. One day, for reasons unknown to us centuries later, the town and its temple are abandoned. The latter loses its power and protection and falls at the mercy of the jungle that, slowly and inexorably, swallows it.

The components of the Unit of Four usually place themselves around and at a distance from the Unit of Two, which usually but not always starts on the platform. Sometimes, one or both Temple people begin off the platform and rise onto it slowly. The Jungle is costumed as vegetation, with *shmattes*, parts of costumes, masks, headpieces, gloves, and plant props. No two costumes have ever been alike. They are to become the plants that are poised to invade but are pushed back from the Temple's sacred space. Theirs will be a very slow forward and backward motion in the space, until the abandonment of the Temple, at which time their engulfing of the architecture will proceed unimpeded. It is obvious from the "story" that the focus will be more on the Temple during the first part of the piece. It seems therefore likely that those who volunteer to play the Jungle are people who are less confident of their work, beginners, or shy performers. The Jungle gives them time and a chance to focus strongly on their personae, on the action, on the Unit, and not worry about "doing it right". I've had a Jungle with a jaguar or a boa in it but that's comparatively rare! Jungle people, depending on what plant they feel they are, will crawl on the ground, or creep around against the back wall, their invasion impeded by invisible machetes.

Portraying the Mayan Temple is a much more difficult task. The costume must be rigid and stone-like, but reminiscent of Mayan gods: feathers, short skirts, elaborate headdresses, jewelry, etc. The performers must portray passive blocks of stone seemingly moved by an outside force. There is a great difference in motion whose impetus comes from the object itself, or by an outside source activating the motion. The first part of the exercise illustrates this difficult technique. In a way, it's a bit like Power at a Distance, with the Power being invisible, yet responded to as if it were actualized.

I consider that there are two kinds of movement. One is *utilitarian*: you move in order to change your position in space. Or, an external force activates you. Or, you are to fulfill a task: picking up, sitting, dragging, sculpting, etc. The muscular and skeletal cooperation needed to fulfill these actions are the only demands of that motion, with no attention to style or choreography. The other kind of movement is for *art's* sake, and often masks the utilitarian and muscular aspect in order to emphasize style and form. In dance, or any other movement stylization, the utilitarian aspect is usually hidden and the art form emphasized. This is demonstrated most famously in Ballet, when the utilitarian gymnastic is camouflaged by the male partner in order to create the illusion that the ballerina floats or flies in the air effortlessly, or when the ballerina moves gracefully on tiny platforms supporting her weight (toes). Achieving these physical feats with seeming ease is the *raison d'être* of that art form. Utilitarian motion was assimilated into dance by the people of the Judson Church group in the 1960s, and has taken many forms since then, with combinations of the two types.

In order to portray the building of the temple, the utilitarian aspect must be masked by the needs of the "story", i.e. the effort of rising from the platform has to be portrayed as originating outside the actual stones, by invisible and imaginary human builders. To portray a utilitarian movement in an artistic way, one must be a highly stylzed form! A difficult combination! Little by little the Temple rises, sometimes the stones are carved with the frightening images of the Mayan gods, their eyes bulging, their tongues sticking out. The motion of the two is a slow, heavy placement of the body and its parts, creating kaleidoscopic views of the rising temple, their eyes in immobile No-Focus Focus, and their balances secured by their partnership.

The section of the piece that is the apogee of the Temple and its time of greatest power and importance demands enormous "presence" and radiation of energy. This can last a while, if the Jungle doesn't begin to encroach! My experience is that, no matter what I say to suggest patience, waiting for the right moment and expressing long passages of time, the Jungle nearly always descends upon the Temple and begins to destroy it too soon. Ideally, there is a period of triumph after the Temple is built, remembering that the Mayan temples were symbols of absolute Power and great cruelty. This pride and apogee lasts a while, the length of time must be felt and determined by the Temple and played out. After a period where only the lights and music express the theme, the unseen people abandon the place, due to war, drought, overpopulation, or other calamity, and the Temple is no longer protected. It begins to lose its power and its majesty. That is the time for the Jungle to begin its *slow* (!) advance, expressing its need for a new scaffold for expansion.

The Temple must exhibit its pain and humiliation, but as stone, not as human! It eventually is brought down, or perhaps left standing as a plinth or pedestal with the Jungle vines coiled around it. The piece often ends with one of the Jungle people rising high above the ruin, alive and victorious, surrounded by the vegetation that covers the fallen stones. The piece can be exciting and effective, especially as the lighting and sound play their dramatic roles to enhance the action. If need be, green gels are substituted for some of the existing color plot before the pieces begin, leaving the golds for the Temple.

The playing of this piece by two different groups is very important. This is the first "total" improvising witnessed by the group, using lights, costumes, a minimal set, and music. We analyze what worked and what didn't, and in what way it could have been made better. Both pieces are thus compared and we learn from both successes and blunders. The students are often amazed at the beauty of the pieces, with strong personifications of non-human entities. The effect is dramatic and exciting. The students are impressed and influenced by what they see, and also encouraged to perform new and even more astonishing feats. They get a chance to do that in the following group improvisation with no theme.

Without theme: "BIOYA"

I call these no-theme group pieces BIOYA or "Blow It Out Your Ass".

The BIOYA is a wonderful exercise, because, among other qualities, if done right it is so satisfying and so good for one's self-esteem! There is nothing more delicious than a good BIOYA! It gives you permission and opportunity to put what you've learned into practice, but not in a mechanical or didactic way. Simply put, you absorb what I taught and make it yours. When there is no theme at the outset, a theme usually develops of its own accord and, after a while, with people paying attention and following a promising lead, the theme establishes itself. Some people are good at bringing forth a theme early on, and the rest of the group must heed it. Often you get a "theme and variations" kind of composition, as the original theme is kneaded into various shapes. The themes may be completely formal, or may put forth content.

Sometimes I have the BIOYA people do it in their workshop clothes, sometimes I ask for costumes. If they are not costumed, it is easier for them to form and dissolve Units, because they are not visually bound to remain together as when their costumes establish that they are a Unit. The best, I believe, is for the entire cast to dress as a Unit, let's say in black or white, or whatever color. Or all wear hats or other distinguishing appendages. The unity of color or detail binds them together if they wish to portray a Unit, and it also binds the piece as a whole, and allows for the Units to split and re-form without being hampered by a very specific individual look.

A large group in a smallish space can be daunting at first, until you realize that two rules must be followed: "Units" and "Entrances and Exits". In other words, the beneficial and always reliable "Units" will put order and organization in the fashioning of the piece.

Entrances and Exits

The "Entrances and Exits" rule consists of entering the stage only when there's a good reason for it, such as a development by players already performing who can use reinforcements or who create a need for more players; or performers on stage who seem to be stuck and need relief; or inspiration that sends you on stage with a new input, a twist, or a quick insert that could refresh the action; or whatever other reason you can think of. This "Entrance" can be a solo, or a Unit, depending on the feel of the moment, as well as the availability of players waiting in the wings. "Exits" happen when the performer feels that his or her contribution has run its course, whether it is short or long. Sometimes an "Entrance and Exit" may just be running through the space and out, or any rapid appearance and disappearance that I would place under the rubric of "Accent" or "Punctuation". This, as the name implies, is a very short contribution to the piece that establishes a visual or vocal accent, a mood, color or emotional statement, perhaps a word, all of which space, indicate, or organize the way they do in written grammar: "Units", "Entrances and Exits", and "Punctuation" are three techniques to remember when doing large group pieces. They can be applied to smaller casts also, and are there to help compose while improvising.

Music

The person on sound has many CDs to choose from, sometimes letting silence take over; other times blending one CD into another. We also sometimes use an air synthesizer, with amazing sounds. In the two days remaining, we will have many more improvised pieces that will be done to live music. We have a collection of drums, flutes, gongs, bells, xylophones and sound-makers of every kind to choose from. Often students bring musical instruments that they play, and either share with others or not. I also have a little upright piano that isn't tuned, and that emits weird tones. Typically, two people will sit on the side of the stage, watching the performers, and playing "music" that will at times support the mood and action, and sometimes exist on a parallel track. Either way, it is important for every student to experience the contribution of all theatrical arts: performing, set-making, costuming, lighting and sound, and get plenty of practice in all these during the weekend.

The Density/Duration Ratio

The Density/Duration Ratio is another one of my "rules". It is about how much you can put into a portion of time, without it being too "thin" or too "thick". If the piece has been assigned 5 minutes or 20 minutes, there is a great difference in the texture of events that fill the short and the long. You must develop a sense of "density" according to "duration", and neither be a glutton nor starve the piece!

ASSIGNMENT

At the end of the evening, I announce that there will be an assignment, to be brought in the next day. It consists of a five-minute solo piece on a subject that usually has to do with the Earth, such as "The Four Elements", "The Seasons", "Time", or any other theme that focuses on the Planet. Or not. "Love" has been a successful theme too! As the solo is being created (during the few moments available between now and tomorrow pm), the students must keep in mind that it is only 50 percent of the stage event, because it will be performed in tandem with another. In other words, each student will be randomly paired with another, and both solos will happen together and simultaneously, on stage. This creates an open-ended approach to individual pieces, adds extra flavors to the brew, and is part planned, part improvised. The existence of another on the stage eases the egocentric approach that sometimes plagues this kind of work. The students are told that they must use No-Focus Focus and be aware of what the partner is up to. They may choose to connect directly, or indirectly. By directly I mean on the same Level, visibly playing to and with the other, or connecting indirectly by maintaining a different Level, but using rhythm, sound, unison, or harmony to effect a total composition and one that can give a seemingly coherent "story" without directly playing a linear narrative together. In a word, the connection can be based on composition, and be abstract.

I ask if there is a need for rides and beds that hasn't been addressed beforehand. People usually find what they need within the group, and if not, they sleep on a pad in my studio. We say Goodnight, the students leave, and the Slaves of Love remain another half-hour to clean up and restore order.

ASSESSMENT OF FRIDAY

When we end the first session on Friday night, people are very tired, but wired. There is excitement, a mood of anticipation. Even though many questions remain floating in the air, most students are happy, and can't wait to continue the work. What I try to do is to leave them, at Friday's end, with enough basic skill, the start of a common vocabulary, and an idea of where we're going as an art form, to be able to approach the work from then on with confidence and aplomb. They have understood the rules, and now need to experiment and experience. Rarely do I get someone who is in the wrong workshop. Sometimes this unfortunate situation is discovered early on, sometimes not. I've had very few students that I evicted, or who quit, perhaps a handful, in the 30 years of teaching DbD. I could count my students in the thousands. I learn from every group, from every individual. No two DbDs are alike. I change things around, I invent new processes, and I explain better, I succeed in calibrating the feedback for fuller effect. I find that the results become more rapid with every workshop. I am happy to notice some very impressive progress in less and less time. I am glad when we can achieve this since speed seems to be a *sine qua non* these days. We jump over many hurdles in the weekend, but without feeling rushed. I try, throughout the work, to encourage people to dare, without worrying about whether they are "good" or not. The important thing is to find out what they are capable of, where there is impediment, what scares them, where they are shy, or overly confident, competitive, vain, ignorant, and anything else about themselves that they can work on without putting themselves down. I also insist on humor and self-humor. It's important that students be able to laugh at themselves and others, and not be afraid of humorous feedback. It is equally important for them to be complimented and admired when there is reason for it. And there should be an atmosphere of serious concentration along with joy. The act of improvising is like the opening of Pandora's box. But it can also be the entrance to Ali-Baba's treasure cave. We must never forget that the goal is predominantly and always the making of *art*. If this target is kept in mind, a lot of excessive misery that comes from self-obsession or self-hatred disappears. That's when true progress is made, both within ourselves and in the work we do.

"Puppets". Photo by Helena Ruffin

"Units". Photo by Helena Ruffin

"Units-2". Photo by Helena Ruffin

"Units and Levels". Photo by Helena Ruffin

BIOYA.. Photo by Jason Jenn

BIOYA. Photo by Jason Jenn

"Hidden Aspect". Photo by Helena Ruffin

Solos as duet. Photo by Jason Jenn

BIOYA. Photo by Rachel Rosenthal

Mayan Temple. Photo by Helena Ruffin

Life Story Solo. Photographer unknown

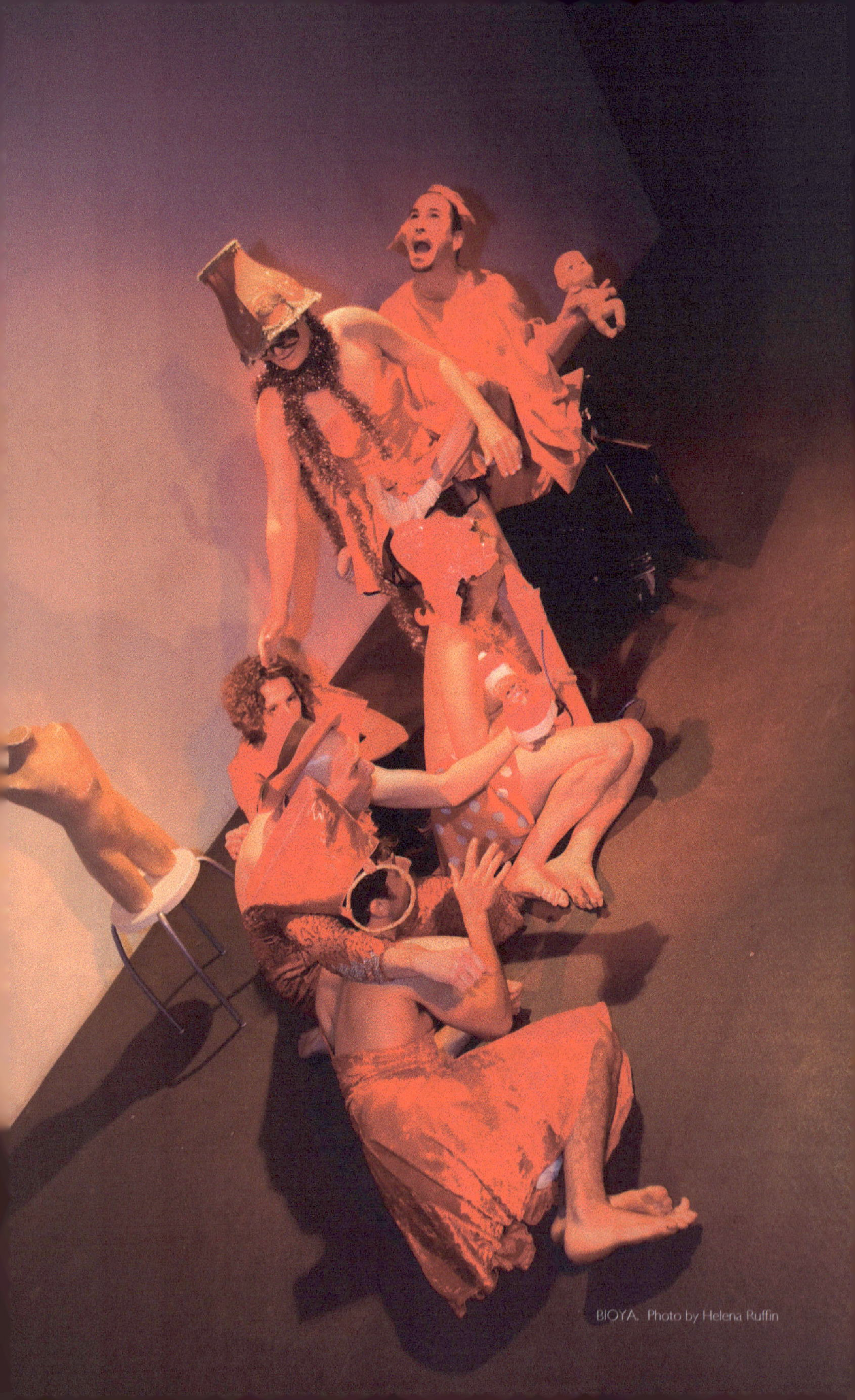

BIOYA. Photo by Helena Ruffin

Saturday: "Connections"

Circle Talk: "Connections"

We sit in a circle, and I improvise my Connections speech.

> Everything is connected to everything else. It should no longer be understood as "six degrees of separation", but as less than six degrees of connection! Sub-atomic physicists have long ago discovered nuclear particles that can communicate in a non-spatial manner, i.e. "talk" to each other across space and vacuums with no means of physical contact whatsoever. This uncanny discovery fueled spiritual beliefs, and emphasized that all of creation is somehow and mysteriously connected.
>
> Nevertheless, a lot of people feel alienated, separate, and alone. How can that be, if there is connection everywhere? It can be, of course, because people create antagonisms between themselves and so many others, human or not, as if their lives depended on it—or actually, their deaths! Since time immemorial, humans have placed Nature in an adversary and hostile stance vis-à-vis themselves, an obvious projection of their own enmity with the natural world. Nature was something to exploit, control, dominate, and recreate as willing victim and slave, that gives of its "renewable resources" until its gifts are exhausted and renewable no more. We condone this attitude and behavior in ourselves the way people condone so-called self-defense murders. "The victim advanced menacingly, with a perceived weapon, so I used my gun!"
>
> Not all humans are Earth haters. Many cultures, uncontaminated by Western Civilization, still exhibit a reverence and love for the Planet that began ages ago. But we of Western Civ do not. We are now paying the price of our

parenticide, and will suffer much in retribution. Already the suffering has begun, as the result of catastrophic natural events like Katrina, tornados, fires, temperature, earthquakes, floods and drought, all more devastating than they ever were within memory, much of it due to climate changes activated and speeded up in great part by our species' greed and ignorance.

Long ago, we saw fit to put a price tag on everything on Earth, starting with pieces of its surface that we exploit, buy or sell. We have also put a price tag on every action, every move we make. As a result, we are transformed into calculators, and everything in our lives has a value—a monetary value. A person who gives of themselves to the planet or other creatures without a price attached is considered somewhat naïve, if not downright stupid. When disasters occur, the media talk about dollars lost, not lives or honor. The suffering of animals is seldom mentioned. But the sensation we call happiness has nothing to do with finances. Each one of us must discover what, in our personal experience, activates the feeling of being happy. In my case, art-making, living with other animals, and the giving of gifts are my personal answer to the secret of achieving happiness. It might not work for others. But the sense of completeness, comfort, and joy that art-making, petting an animal, and gift-giving brings, works for me.

People who create usually seek solitude and silence. But that is not necessarily true of all artists. Bob Rauschenberg used to paint with a radio blaring, and many people turn on their CD player, and now, their iPod. Since the advent of cell phones, almost everyone we see is constantly speaking to someone else at the other end. Cell phones answered a vital need for constant connection, for the feeling of never being alone. It gives us the illusion of closeness, and the virtual connection exists only in e-land. Cell phones now also provide entertainment to distract us from our angst.

The truth is that we are never alone. The electronic illusion of togetherness may not be the answer to the search for happiness. We are like a knot in a long knotted string. This string, actually, is more like a spider's web, branching out in every direction, and into three and four dimensions too. Perhaps more. All these knots, on the continuum of our web, represent people, events, places, thoughts, memories, affinities, clans or tribes, all the entities and events that have formed who we are and who we are becoming. We are repositories. Each one of us is a treasure trove that should be mined and archived. We have access to our history in all its aspects and depth, to connect with and use, as needed, in our art. However, beware of doing theater pieces that set yourselves up as central and unique to the content. In my solo work, I used my past as metaphor for global issues. Thus satisfying two compelling components of solo work: the digging into universal issues, and the use of autobiography as a bridge to make it accessible to an audience's sensibility.

I imagine that, before we developed speech, we had far closer ties with the individuals of our clan and the manifestations of Nature. I also imagine that a lot of communication was done by touch, gesture, and facial expression, in addition to voice. Then, after body language, came language. Language is a great separator. Words categorize and identify individuals, be they human or not, whole or in parts. They separate things more effectively than fences. Eventually, words also separate ideologies, beliefs, and preferences, create prejudices and intolerance, and put up semantic walls between us. And words can lie.

For instance, a "*Tree*" is not just the green foliage on a trunk that children learn to paint as a round green lollipop on a brown stick. It is so many other things as well: a whole world underground, full of organisms that break down the soil to allow the roots to access food and water; it is the home of countless insects who live, eat, propagate and die in its trunk; it is the home of birds, mammals, parasites, reptiles—some who are predators, some prey—who keep the cycle of life and death churning. The leaves are in constant connection with the sun and the air, absorbing nutrients, ejecting gasses, keeping the atmosphere on an even keel, replenishing air with the necessary balance that will sustain life, keeping oxygen at a level that won't incinerate the Earth. The tree will regulate temperature, stabilize climate, and insist also on being beautiful, putting out lovely flowers, sometimes edible fruit, and providing shade for those who crave it. Take away any of those attributes, and you no longer have a "Tree".

Origins and Connections are two very important concepts that can be useful to us, both in art and in life. Origins anchor us within the Cosmos in a conscious way, and so does Connections, which helps us situate ourselves within the biology and geology of the Planet. One can imagine Origins as dealing with Time, and Connections as dealing with Space—in a perhaps simplistic way, but, remembering that Einstein coined the concept "Space/Time", we can feel the unity of all things terrestrial as well as human, in this manner.

Dogs

TohDoh the dog participates in an improv.
Photo by Helena Ruffin

By the time we reach the second day, the dogs have made ample appearances in the studio. People usually welcome them with enthusiasm. The dogs are polite, have the protocol down, and behave better in a theater situation than many a spectator we have had to tolerate at some point in time. When they do rise from napping on a cushion and join the action on stage, it usually happens either during set-making between pieces, or when the students are all lying sprawled over the floor for a process that requires it. They sniff, visit, lie down next to some people, stay a while and then go back to the audience cushions and take another nap. They usually understand that any yelling or untoward noise is part of the "play", and rarely spook, only if the action and sound get very brutal or menacing. They usually figure it out, or, discreetly, exit. The energy they put out is sweet, patient, friendly, and beneficial. It seems to have a very healing effect on people, those who are familiar with inter-species relationships, and those who aren't. I find those moments to be very important to the development of the weekend, and welcome them without interfering. They are fleeting and release tension. When the students are sitting on cushions in the spectator area, they often find themselves close to a dog. As they watch and listen, they absentmindedly pet the dog, place their hands on the dog's fur, and simply connect physically for a while. This touch seems to underscore my belief that a lot of the success of my workshops comes from my actively pursuing conscious and unconscious connections to the Planet's Nature in all its forms. Being close to an animal of another species helps achieve this link.

NATURE AND US

It was around five decades ago that I became very concerned about what was happening on and to the Earth. I had been living in a wooded area of the Hollywood Hills, with many dogs and cats. At that time, in the 1950s and 1960s, I began to read literature concerning the problems of our environment, as well as the horrors of vivisection, cosmetic testing, the food animals industry, and other abominations. These concerns seemed to me urgent, and needing immediate attention. I noticed that hardly anyone was heeding them, except for the writers, researchers and scientists dedicated to these issues. I began to bring the subjects up during question and answer sessions after performances and lectures, and in my workshops. Still, nothing seemed obvious or urgent to the public at that time, the media deemed the subject not important enough for the first page or the evening news, and so the status quo remained. Unfortunately, we were reaching the point of no return in our overpopulation, meat consumption, pollution, deforestation, desertification, ozone damage, climate change, loss of drinking water and arable land, over-fishing, over-grazing, and the multiple extinctions caused mostly by habitat loss, hunting, fishing, poaching, and disregard of the needs of other populations, as well as the release of toxic gases and waste all over the planet. Apparently these very real problems were not bad enough to arouse the population or our government. I was viewed as a Cassandra, and I felt isolated and alone in my passionate warnings. Of

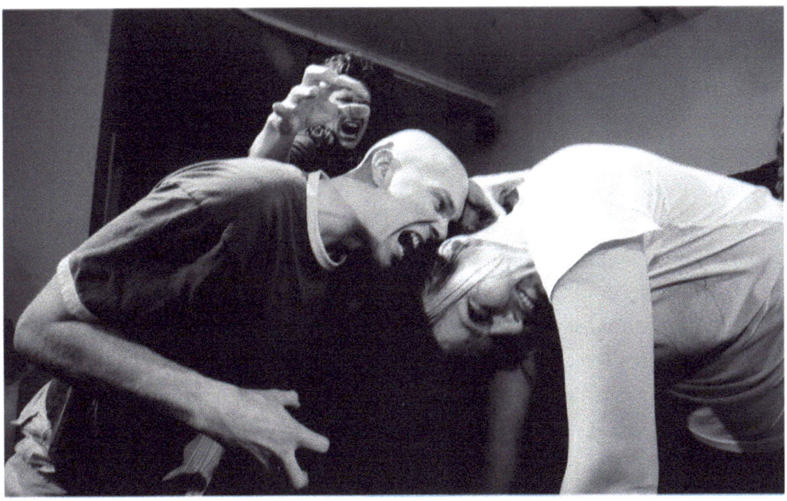

Tableau: lions feeding. Photo by Helena Ruffin

course, it had to reach a point where the media would have to sit up and take notice. It did. In the beginning of the third millennium, five decades later! Well, I guess better late than never! Still, the point of no return had been reached and passed, and if anything was to change, urgent and draconian steps should have been taken immediately. It is too late now for change and arrested disaster, but not too late for adjustment and attenuation. A lot of people think so and trust our technological achievements. We are altering the Planet irrevocably, in any case, and can say goodbye to Earth as we've known it. Will we have the vision needed to make the necessary sacrifices that might save us from planetary disaster?

Companion animals are another question. Much progress in our treatment and understanding of such animals has already occurred. But there are still great quantities of horrendous cruelties inflicted, and ignorance displayed in every country, in spite of the realizations and actions of some individuals, organizations and communities that have studied animals both wild and domesticated, educated themselves, changed their behavior, and who propagate intelligent new ways of seeing the animals and acting on their behalf.

I am a vegetarian, and proselytize for vegetarianism. In addition to the now obvious human health reasons for not consuming animals, there is a moral obligation for doing so, because of the deplorable conditions under which food animals are bred and killed. The short lives of billions of mammals, birds, and sea creatures, are ones of endless torture, and their deaths are horrific. How can we ethically justify eating these creatures? More and more information is surfacing regarding both the consciousness of non-human animals, their ability to feel, think, suffer, and communicate their emotions and understanding, in addition to their genetic closeness to our own constitutions. We are enslaving, tormenting, and slaughtering our close relatives, in many cases, and then ingesting them, in what many others and I regard as cannibalism! Food is pushed, in this society, as fashionable, and often as emblematic of class. You've heard of trophy wives, there is also trophy food. And boutique food! Advertisement is difficult to avoid and resist. And yet, in addition to our obvious fat as visible result of our wrong eating, much information is constantly surfacing regarding the dangers of meat-eating and the toxicity of many popular foods that must be forcibly yanked from market shelves, the animals they are made of murdered en masse when, as living beings, they are deemed dangerous to humans. We are omnivorous and do not need animal protein in order to be healthy. Eliminating animals from our diets not only would be good for our bodies, but also would cut down on the immense overuse of energy, water and arable land, and on the pollution and destruction of huge portions of nature on this planet, due to factory farming and the food industry in general. We rob wildlife of their habitat, their hunting and mating grounds, their water and nourishment, and we induce extinctions that are the inevitable results of modern husbandry. A time will surely come when eating and exploiting animals will be considered emblematic of our primitive and barbaric civilization, and will be abhorrent to future human beings.

In my workshop, I talk about the importance of seeing these "Other" animals as conscious, intelligent, sentient beings possessing thought and emotional lives. We need to understand that our behavior vis-à-vis these others is a dead-on indication of who we are as people. It is vital that humans take responsibility and get involved in the propagation of respect, understanding, good treatment and protection of non-human animals, and to recognize when to interfere in their affairs and when to just leave them alone and not encroach on their physical and emotional territories. Most animals on this Earth have survived far longer stretches of time than the few thousand years of human existence, and without our help. If we didn't encroach upon them, they could no doubt continue to adjust to changing climates and geographies, and would not die off in the huge numbers and the speed that we have forced upon them. For artists to use or display animals without this understanding, compassion and empathy is odious and must be exposed and stopped. Animal use in any kind of entertainment situation that coerces them (including art) must be abolished. Circuses, and "animal acts" that use brutal training methods, or not, among them. Dog fighting, at last out in the light of day, is outraging citizens, and laws are being drafted to outlaw it. But it still exists. People are fighting our government's insistence on exploiting gas and oil reserves in the last wild areas of our land, resulting in the extinction of many large and small mammals, including ungulates and polar bears. The importance of bringing up these issues in a workshop for experimental theater is not immediately apparent. But, in a mysterious way, I attribute the transformations I observe in my students to their awakening to the "big picture" and to their own connection with my dogs in particular on a microcosmic level, and with Nature as a whole on a macrocosmic level.

The Blob

This is a movement meditation. I give the instructions beforehand and don't interfere verbally during its performance.

The music is Steve Reich's *Drumming*. The sound starts with a drum pulse followed by more, widely spaced. Throughout the piece, which lasts approximately 28 minutes, the drumming accelerates and the amount of instruments rises until

continued

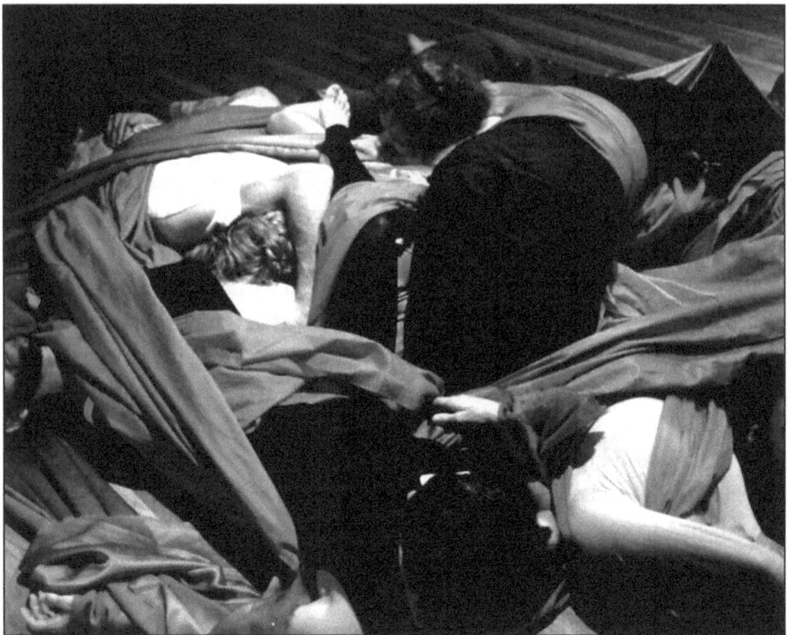

"The Blob". Photo by Rachel Rosenthal

a full percussion orchestra beats out a complex and intricate rhythm over the initial pulse. The lights begin very dim, and slowly become brighter along with the rising complexity of the music.

The Blob instructions

You are unicellular organisms forming a colony at the bottom of the ocean, 500 million years ago. You are forming a pileup with several long *shmattes* woven through it, around bodies, arms, legs, that tie you even more closely with the people under or over you. (Make sure that knees and chests are protected and not weighted down.) You have no face, no appendages, and no digestive tract. You feed over the entire body. As the drums establish a rhythmic drone, motion in any part of the blob will travel throughout the pile-up, and cause organisms across the pile to respond in like manner. The whole blob may look like the contents of an agitated bowl of Jell-O! But the call of evolution begins to be felt and you are caught between the need for

> differentiation, and the instinct to remain within the blob colony. On a human level it would equate to the need to separate versus separation anxiety. Those are two opposite forces and you experience both. If you succeed in differentiating, you can grow a digestive system with food entering from one end and waste ejected at the other end. You can grow appendages with which to catch prey and push it down into your mouth. You can continue your evolution, become more and more complex and intricate, growing eyes and vision, moving onto land, flying. You can stop evolving wherever is your comfort, or continue diversifying into various other species.

Obviously, this exercise is about "connections". However, it is also about how hard it is to connect, and how the impulses of individuation and connecting are both present, albeit opposite, in our history and personal experience. It is also about the difficulty of changing from a simple organism to the highly evolved ones that came later. It is a way of connecting on a very primitive level with an amazing saga of effort, metamorphosis, and relationship. It also brings the realization of consciousness existing on the lowest rungs of the food chain, and up.

There are many such exercises during the weekend, that reach into the far past and the far future, in order to relate to our history, both physiological and mental, to appreciate and access the organisms and organs that we take for granted. These exercises also suggest expressing, through movement, states that are difficult to inhabit, and allow the body to explore new ways of moving that will induce a participant to penetrate states that retain their secret, their mystery, and to touch areas of feeling and understanding that were dormant and ignored. Eyes are closed for the most part, and as people move around on the floor, bodies are touched. It is important that there be no explicitly sexual touches, or that hands not linger inappropriately on sensitive parts of the body. That may be distracting and disturbing. This can be stated before the exercise begins, in a simple and unembarrassed way.

Connections Dance

In as seamless a manner as possible, I have the students switch from the "Blob" exercise to a "Connections Dance", a movement piece whose music emanates from the Steve Reich piece but goes beyond percussion into tonal harmony. Without pulling the people away too suddenly from their Blob trance, I have them transform their movement into a slow dance where everyone is always physically connected to at least one other person. As the group evolves in slow motion, I have them accentuate their touch into something more demanding, giving and taking

Flying during "Connections Dance". Photo by Kate Noonan

weight. There is an effort to create a group piece that is slow, harmonious, and that uses others in the way that acrobats do, with difficult balances achieved through connecting muscularly and using others for equilibrium. I slowly guide them verbally to begin lifting bodies off the floor. I tell them that they will need several lifters, and that they should instantly *be where needed*, under an airborne body that is sagging, for example. Wherever the pull of gravity seems to win out, that's where they should be, countering the pull. In this manner, bodies are "flown", high up, across the floor, several people to one body, the number depending on the weight of the "flyer" and the strength of the lifters. This teaches the players to notice where their contribution is to occur, quickly and efficiently. There should be no inner deliberation about these things, but an instant assessment of the situation, a quick move to be where there is a gap, and to participate until the grouping dissolves and another grouping forms. Let the body instinct and knowledge take over. Thus, all experience "flying", but more importantly, all experience the body reflex of instantaneous right action. They become able to go beyond the stage of reflection before action, and are there not a split second too late. The exercise also continues to develop in the participants a regard for other bodies beside their own.

TECHNICALS

After "The Blob", there is a session for learning the light board and familiarizing students with the collection of props, costumes, and musical objects. If there are twelve people, six will learn the board while the other six go to the Props and Costumes Room. Either the Slaves of Love or I teach the light board, depending on who the Slaves are and if they have sufficient experience and proficiency. Before we split up, I talk to the students about lights and props and costumes.

Lights

I am devoted to lighting. It is 50 percent of the performance, in my view. Lights paint the stage and create half the "story" by establishing the mood, style, and focus to the piece. There are many plays, dances, or performance works that I remember through their lighting while the rest is forgotten. The lighting person has enormous power and responsibility. She or he sets the atmosphere at the start of the piece and, most importantly, decides when and how to end it. There are many ways to go to blackout: it can be slow and gradual for the entire plot; it can occur by dimming out every lamp, one by one, until only one is left, lighting and finally blacking out the main action; it can be slow or sudden, its rhythm and timing vitally important to the way an audience is left after experiencing the piece. Of course you need a board that is not operated by computer because, since the work is improvisational, there is no way to plan or plot the lighting in advance, as one does with a computerized board. However, manually operated boards have become scarce, and often non-existent in most venues. This is a very real obstacle to free improvisation, and why I like to keep its experience in my studio.

The lighting person must dance internally with the performers, anticipate where they go in the space, underline important moments or unfocus certain others, and has the power to change the action by shifting mood and placement. At a light board that lets you improvise with the stage event, your fingers do the walking, and you must be very aware and sensitive to the contrast between the small distance the fingers travel and the huge effect of that motion on the stage. Your fingers must learn how to be subtle or blunt, and it is a continual dialogue in space between the board and the action.

It is also necessary for the performers on stage to know their lights and play with them. Don't perform important scenes in areas of the stage that are badly lit. Find your lights. When you do, make sure you are right in the "hot spot", and that the shaft of light centers where you want it, on your face, presumably. Like a moth, you must feel the heat of the light attracting you. The performers and the person on the board, in a kind of dialogue in space, share responsibility for good lighting. Each student is given a few minutes to acquaint themselves with the board, as others move in the space as models for focusing.

Props and Costumes

Before they're taken to the Props and Costumes Room, the students are told that they will have no more than four minutes to dress and create the set for a piece or exercise. As soon as they have volunteered or been assigned to be in the piece, the clock starts to tick. The set makers run to fetch objects from the wings and place them on stage. The players rush to the Props and Costumes Room. The way we enter that room is critical. There is to be no giggling or gossiping. Don't scatter your energy in meaningless ways. The students must be completely focused on the objects, and if they achieve a light trance, they will find that bits of costumes seem to jump up and adorn them of their own volition! It is also vital that a No-Focus-Focus gaze be maintained in order to monitor others and what they are

Props and Costumes Room. Photo by Kate Noonan

wearing, as they prepare to be in the same piece. A wordless harmony must be established. Unity of costuming opens the way for Units, and gives the piece, no matter how many performers are in it, a visual harmony that satisfies. Again, a clash may be desired and needed, and that too can be visually achieved by taking note of what others are wearing. The costume worn is then examined in large mirrors. The reflected image is that of the persona, a second skin, one that can be tweaked and completed with smaller details such as props. The reflected image tells you who or what you are, how to move as such, and what dramatic path you might take to activate this persona.

It is also crucial that the students notice where things belong before they hurriedly grab them. When the piece is done and the feedback has been given, the student is responsible for returning each item to its rightful place. There is very little time for costuming and, if items are not put back, there can be a search for a desired specific costume or prop that has disappeared from its assigned place. This wastes precious time and can throw the students' performance badly. So remember where things belong! The students begin to experiment with costumes and props for the remaining minutes.

After getting acquainted with the technicals we go back to work.

VOICE

Posture

The students sit in a circle on the floor. They are to straighten their spine, and to thrust their pelvis back so that their buttocks stick out, as if they had a "duck's tail". The stomach is not pulled in, but allowed to relax. I have them do that and then relax their lower spine (coccyx), without thrusting the pelvis out in the duck's tail, to demonstrate how that allows the spine to droop, whereas the duck's tail automatically pulls up all the vertebrae into a straight vertical line. At the top of the neck, vertebrae support the skull, and at the top of the skull is an imaginary string that pulls the whole back upward. I then have them relax their shoulders while keeping erect, and I ask them to take their hand and place it on their profile, gently pushing the head back (not up or down) in the way of Buddhist meditation, so as to prevent the face from dragging the head and neck forward, as it sometimes does.

Head Roll

Note: My ex-husband King Moody, who learned it at the Academy of Dramatic Arts in New York City, showed this head roll to me. It is very effective. This is my version of it.

In the sitting position described above, the students go into No-Focus Focus and slowly let their eyelids drop, closing the eyes. They then open their mouths and stick out their tongues, activating the muscles of the mouth. Next, they relax the tongue, letting it rest on the lower teeth and lip. The neck muscles then relax too, letting the head drop onto the chest. The tongue will be out of the mouth during the entire exercise. The head roll begins, and the students are asked to let it last between five and ten minutes. The slowness of the roll is vital, forcing the students to relax completely, and to align themselves with a time frame that quiets nerves, impatience, worry, disturbing thoughts, etc. It produces a slight trance, and prepares for focus, centering, and places consciousness into the body. I ask the students not to lead with their noses when the head reaches the shoulder, but rather with their ear, as when the head rests on a pillow at night. When the head comes to the back, I remind them to open their mouths even more to let the tongue out fully, as this releases the neck muscles and allows the head to fall back as far as possible. They should cheat their posture back slightly so as to allow the neck and head to fall backward of their own weight unimpeded, not "placed" there by thinking. The head continues to move from the back to the other shoulder. That part of the exercise is usually the most painful as so much present and past ache is lodged and retained in that area of neck, back, and shoulder. Dragging the head around over those places releases much tension and causes suffering. Some people cry, from either pain or release. Finally, the head moves down from the shoulder, lead by the opposite ear, and rests back again on the chest. Of course, the slower the exercise is done, the better. Some people race through it and have to repeat it several times before they manage to slow down enough. I ask them to think of the hands of a clock, whose motion is invisible, yet they move.

To come out of this exercise, the group is told to keep their mouths open and eyes closed, and to activate the head into quick circles, not by placing (again!), but from the impulses of the torso. The back and torso muscles whip the neck around, and the head moves in fast turns, in one direction, then another.

Breath

Sitting in that posture the students must do three full breaths, emptying out completely on each exhale. I then demonstrate how I want their breath performed: I give them a count of six in, and six out. On the first 1, 2, 3, they are to inhale and dilate their abdomen, so that the stomach (*not* the breast) sticks out. This action lowers the diaphragm, making more space for air in the lungs. On the 4, 5, 6, with the stomach dilated, the back part of their ribs should dilate also, thus opening even more room in the lungs. I call it the "Fish's Gills". On the exhale, 1, 2, 3, the stomach pulls in, pushing the diaphragm up toward the lungs while the ribs are still pushing out, and on 4, 5, 6, the ribs press against the lungs in the back, emptying what's left of the breath, thus allowing the performer a "second wind". I then create a beat with my hand on my knee, counting the numbers out loud while they practice this breathing, and after two such breaths, I augment the count to 8, then 10, and 12. This forces the students to breathe and exhale to a count, getting slower with each one, and teaching how to obtain longer breaths, while still not displaying any visible "heaving" frontally.

Vocal Chord Vibration ("Purring")

We then go to the first vocal exercise. This "Purring" is the clicks sound that vocal cords make when they are vibrating but not creating "voice". This is a characteristic sound differing from a "note" or any kind of vocal output such as talking or singing. Its purpose is mainly to open the throat and relax the vocal cords, and is very useful before a performance. You take a deep breath (as above), and then begin to produce this sound, like a tiger's energetic purr, mouth open. The slower the vibrations (clicks further apart, that one can separate and count), the more relaxed the throat (the purpose of the exercise). There is no effort whatsoever in this process. It's like a puncture in a tire. Once the puncture gets under way, the air simply escapes at its own pace, slowly oozing out without being pushed, vibrating the vocal cords as it goes. If there is effort, it usually produces a vocal sound, which, coupled with the vibrations, produces a growl. That's a good sound to remember, but mustn't be confused with the purr.

Vibration into Sound

The following exercise is for students to experience the production of voice sound. The preparation is as before, and the "purring" begins. About half way through the breath, the throat and the management of the column of air shifts, and from vibration, the vocal chords are asked to create a sound, a good, strong, long note (only one!). The "purr" is lost. Eventually the note will be pulled back and replaced by the purring vibration before fading away. I always tell my students to feel what is happening to voice production in this exercise, because I don't know how to describe and explain it in words. I demonstrate, and it has to be felt. It is not difficult to do, but from this simple exercise stem the many voice extensions, placement, and diction that are part of our sound vocabulary.

Voice Placement

There are many kinds of voice placements, pertaining to different cultures. The voice can be placed very low in the abdomen—as in certain Asian chanting—in the chest, in the throat, in various parts of the mouth, up in the nasal cavities, in the cheeks, in the head. The usual Western European placement, and the one that is favored by theater actors and classical and opera singers, is in the front of the mouth, the column of air hitting the back of the upper teeth. It sounds complicated but isn't. If you close your mouth, not tightly but enough so that your lips touch lightly, you know you've hit the spot when your lips begin to vibrate and to tickle, sometimes vigorously. This indicates that the column of air, in the right placement, is pushing the lips open for the sound to emerge. At this point, you open your mouth, *without altering the pitch of the note*, or the placement of the column of air, and out comes a lovely sound, with the desired intensity of projection. This is how opera voices attain such volume, or how spoken text can be heard from the balcony without microphones. Volume is attained by the action of torso and abdomen muscles, and the chest muscles should not be seen heaving or pushing. The things to look for and correct are the change of pitch between the time the lips are closed and the mouth opens, and the shift in placement, both due to a change in the musculature of the closed-to-open action of the mouth. We are working to achieve control over our vocal apparatus, and lack of control should be corrected at once.

> Note: All the above Voice Exercises are variations of the ones taught me by King Moody.

Variation on "Voice Circle". Photo by Kate Noonan

Voice Circle

At this point, I work one on one with each student. I sit in front of them on the floor, and have them do the exercise by themselves as I monitor and correct their performance. This set-up is very scary for people, the proud ones as well as the shy ones. They are alone, the focus of attention, called on to perform for the instructor who is in their face.

I set it up this way for those very reasons, because performing can be very frightening, and fear brings out all the issues we need to deal with, conquer, and go beyond, in order to gain from the experience and progress in the workshop.

Many people have been voice-traumatized as children: told they must be "seen but not heard", told they can't sing, have no ear or musical sense, told to "shut up", not to scream, that they're too loud, etc. Those old tapes keep playing throughout their lives and prevent them from using an organ that, if left to develop normally, allows everyone to sing, do voice extensions, shout, speak to be heard, etc. If blocked, much effort goes, in later life, to unblock this vital part of our performing instrument.

First, I address their gaze. A lot of people forget to use No-Focus Focus, and, as a result, try to avert looking and seeing, or making eye contact with anyone in the circle, including me. Their gaze is down or up, but not level. Or their eyes are closed. When that is corrected, I need to quiet whatever nervous twitch or gesture they use as barrier, be it hands, feet, smile, posture, or whatever. I sometimes use the Gamelan example, presenting as role models Indonesian musicians who sit on the floor, backs straight, eyes front and level, immobile until they come to life on their instrument, and then go back to a calm image between playing. I make sure all students use the breath correctly, and then I have them produce the one note with proper placement. At this point, many things can happen. People will wiggle, giggle, shift, cough, make false starts, begin explaining or verbalizing excuses, and display all the infinite variations of fear and avoidance. Some even cry.

During this, I am driving on automatic, letting my instincts absolutely free. I might bully, joke, be empathetic, motherly, or house-masterly, be a drill sergeant, all depending on what it is that channels through me, evoked by what's before me. What is most needed for the individual sitting in front of me is what emerges. I ferret out what is behind the fear. I find things like grief, upbringing, pride, anger, self-deprecation, a whole number of impediments. When I feel confident that I've "got" it, I usually come closer, grab the person's hands, and have them forget the exercise and, instead, let out the sound of fear, or grief, whatever, or I make them be disgusting or disgusted, or snobbish, or needy or pornographic, or whatever is hidden and repressed. It is done through sound, and they must crash through the sound barrier to be successful in this exercise. Our greatest inhibitions are in our voices. If I can completely relax, every person in that circle will get the moment of realization that is theirs, and will come out of the exercise with self-confidence, and sometimes a great voice that surprises everyone including the individual in question. I insist on involving the entire body in this exercise, and make sure the person is in the now, in the moment, and not in the burden of the past or the anxiety of the future. I often ask the rest of the group to participate. Sometimes the whole class is bawling loud and clear, or screaming with fear, or roaring in anger or growling aggressively, or dry-heaving disgust, etc. The person before me is no longer alone, the center of attention. All are on an equal level. It liberates the individual and rids her or him of that fear of "not doing it right". As I go around the circle, sitting in front of each in turn, I make sure that I am totally present, drinking in the person in front of me, being absolutely in the instant with each. That way, I am able to get into the person's being and feel what it is that makes them who they are. It's a question of bare honesty. The person in front of me sheds, little by little, the persona that society has created and the real being begins to emerge. I go into this process with the full understanding of the gravity of this exercise, and of my responsibility to each and every student involved, even if humor and good humor prevail. I feel bad when I know that I missed the magical process with one or other of the participants, either through my fault—didn't find the key, didn't wait to hear the "voice", so to speak—or through the opacity of the person whose defenses are too developed to be penetrated at this point. Sometimes, during the weekend, I experience a failure to reach someone, but the mysterious opening may come as part of the next exercise, or another down the road (in some people, it comes about after the weekend is over). When the little moments of success happen, everyone rejoices. It's a communal victory of sorts, and the individual's achievement seems to encompass us all. The last note sung by the student, after having gone through the catharsis, is clear as a bell, produced with confidence and calm, and usually sustained far longer than the initial one. I often have them offer it as a gift to the circle, with a gesture of giving, while focusing on each face in turn, as the beautiful note travels all around. After everyone in the circle has done the exercise, I go back to my seat, and ask for a chorus of long notes, drones, mostly in unison, with a minimal amount of harmony, and it may develop spontaneously into a chant of closeness and emotional release.

ADDITIONAL VOICE EXERCISES

Unison

I go around the circle, assigning each student to be a voice soloist, improvising a short melody (one to two minutes), while the two students on each side sing in unison with that person. All three are to have right posture, gaze ahead of them, not looking at the soloist, and attempt to be as close in timing to full unison as possible. With practice, the breathing of all three is coordinated, and the three voices are as one. Everyone in the circle gets to do a solo, and all do the exercise twice, as members of the Unit of Two, and as soloist. Again, the soloist is in the middle, the two singing in unison are on each side.

Duets

I assign the duets to people on opposite sides of the circle, facing each other across the way. They are to improvise a short voice piece that holds together with beginning, middle and end, also around one to two minutes long. Here, melody and harmony may come in, and unison. What is important is that both are on the same level, without one taking the lead. They must listen to each other, try to form a mutual style, and create a piece with a satisfying musical composition. This may be very difficult for those who don't know how to listen, or who have spent their lives believing they have "no ear". They are afraid of music, uncomfortable, clueless. Alas, so many people have been told that they couldn't "sing", that it has become a self-fulfilling prophecy. I try to assure them that they do indeed have music, but it must be allowed out after years of imprisonment. Some people can't tell if they are in unison or not. They hear pretty music and don't know they are harmonizing. I also ask those people to practice singing in unison with a radio or CD player, or whatever other new technology plays music for them, at home or in their car. Eventually, they will hear when they are in unison or not. The duets go around the circle until all have participated.

Duets with Movement

Two people on opposite sides of the circle are to do a short sound piece, but this time, with movement. Here is an opportunity for bringing the voice into the whole body, and to express not only with music or sound, but also with motion and gesture. Here they may touch, use each other's bodies, roll on the floor, jump up, and explore the use of breath when both the voice and the body are involved. The piece may be started from their sitting position and continue in the center of the circle, or they may start in the center, as they wish.

Combos

Finally, we get into "Combos". "Combos" are a very simple way of organizing improvised bands, using only voice (a cappella), but learning the different roles that the voice can play in a group situation.

I ask for five people, and divide them into Beat (or Pulse), Drone, Rhythm, Melody, and Harmony. They place themselves from back to front: Beat and Drone, standing in the back row; Rhythm and Harmony kneeling in the second row; Melody sitting cross-legged in the front. Another way is Beat and Rhythm standing in the back, Drone kneeling in front of them, Harmony and Melody sitting in front. These positions emphasize the sounds differently and can both be experienced in order to feel how positioning can influence the sound piece.

It begins in the following order: the Beat comes first (d-DA, d-DA, d-DA, d-DA . . . for instance). It is a very simple repetition of a pulse, but must not decelerate or accelerate during the piece. I point out that intervals between beats must always be the same. Keep the intervals short, and make sure you don't lengthen or shorten them.

Next, the Rhythm picks up the Beat and makes it more complex by creating "embroideries" around it. I compare the relationship between the Beat and the Rhythm to the Caduceus, the wand carried by Hermes/Mercury, in Greco-Roman art and religion. The Beat is the baton, vertical and rigid. Around the baton there are two snakes intertwined. That's the Rhythm. The snakes move, but remain essentially dependent on the stick (Beat) they are carried on. Here we may have many kinds of counterpoint and other embellishments to the Beat.

The Drone comes next and establishes a long note, repeated throughout, which should preferably set the key. If it is not used as such, it should be subsequently harmonized with, in such a way as to allow a key to emerge. The Drone should be in the lower register, and gives the piece body and depth, "thickens the soup", so to speak. The note can shift with the harmonics of the composition.

Then comes the Melody, aware of both key and rhythm, who must be able to improvise without being drawn into unison with any of the other musicians. The Melody soars above it all, but remains in key, and may use the Rhythm as its trellis to grow on.

Last, the Harmony creates aural depth for the piece. The Harmony can go with any of the other musicians, in unison, counterpoint, or harmony. But it *must* remain in key. I am aware of contemporary compositions that do not use key. But I insist on it at this stage of the work with my students in order to develop "ear" and avoid chaos, muddiness, and lack of control. The Harmony also expresses different moods and feelings that the melody alone can't communicate. If elucidation of the role of harmony is needed here, it is useful to choose a note and harmonize it with a key chord in both sharp and flat, to demonstrate how harmony alters mood, sharp being "happy" and flat being "sad". Either a student with musicianship can illustrate, or a keyboard, if available, can be played. Creating an improvised five-person Combo is a difficult task for those with no musical background. But after a few attempts, some lovely little pieces may occur. It is important to stress how much awareness and attention must go into the effort.

"Solo with Combo". Photo by Kate Noonan

Solos with Combos

Now the students get to play with instruments. On an empty stage, there is a microphone. All the students in turn get to improvise a solo sound piece, accompanied by a combo of three people, who have each chosen one or several instruments or sound-makers from the Music Booth. The three musicians are a unit due to the fact that they are creating a sound piece together, and supporting the soloist. They can place themselves anywhere in the space, but I find it best when they form a tight grouping. The Soloist gets into position during a blackout and begins the piece in the dark. Next come the lights. This moment allows the combo to hear where the soloist is going, musically. Then the combo begins to play, creating an ensemble, supporting and accompanying the Soloist. The latter performs a piece that may be anywhere from one to three minutes, give or take. The sound must be voice, not whistles, clucks, or any other mouth or percussive sound that doesn't use voice. That's a rule. The voice and the piece as a whole must come from deep feelings or emotional expression, and may use whatever voice extensions will best serve them. There is no language, of course. Breath is a vital component as emotional and expressive motor. The body may move minimally, so long as it doesn't take focus away from the voice, it may participate in order to place emphasis on the content of the piece. The microphone enlarges the effect of the voice and makes even very soft tones audible. It also gives the performer a sense of power and uniqueness. It goes without saying that the piece is wholly improvised and doesn't use any known tune. Often, the piece has no tune at all, and goes into screams, grunts, gargles, squeaks, etc. The soloists usually find this exercise extremely useful. It opens large the doors that were set ajar in the Voice Circle. A great feeling of release ensues, that allows the student to go more boldly into the remaining exercises. Meanwhile, if the combo is successful, there is no separation between the soloist and the Unit of Three. The sound piece is bound together through sound and music.

After this is usually a good place to break for lunch.

ASSIGNMENT

Two Simultaneous Solos on an Earth Theme

The pairing is random. As the students sit in a line in the "audience" section against the wall, I have the first and last of them perform together, then the second and next to last, etc. until all the pairs have taken their turn. Or I ask for volunteers, which of course introduces the element of choice.

The students sometimes bring in a CD of the music they've included in their piece, and give the tech person their cues and directions. They tell their needs to the set person (a volunteer). Usually, each participant stakes out one side of the stage, but at times, one of the sets will take up more than half of the stage. These unexpected "givens" are dealt with instantaneously.

"Eyes Out!"

In my studio, there is no front curtain. Because of my consideration for the audience, I want the spectators to have the surprise of the image the stage sends out with the opening of a curtain at the beginning of a piece. Just as the performers haven't seen the set before they are out of the Props and Costumes Room and ready to take their place on stage, so the audience hasn't seen the costumed players. Hence we have something we call "Eyes Out!" When the performers leave the Props and Costumes room after the maximum four-minute costuming and set-making time, someone yells "Eyes out!" and everyone in the audience (including me) closes their eyes. The set is lit, and the players enter and place themselves standing in front of the audience, with their backs to it. From this vantage point, they gaze at the set, seeing it for the first time from the audience's point of view and assess and make mental notes as to playing areas, dangerous curves, uses the set can be put to according to their planned piece, etc. Sometimes also last-minute set-ups are in order, such as positions that the performer needs a helper to get into, or having someone wrap or hide them in ways that can't be done without outside help; or perhaps the placement of a surprise prop and set piece that should be hidden from the audience for a full effect later on. This is achieved in record time, as the lighting person waits. When the players feel that they "know" enough to play the set, they take position in it, or in the wings, as they wish. When both participants are in place and motionless, the lights dim to black. A couple of beats, and the music begins in the blackout. That is the signal for the audience to open their eyes. At that point, the lights come up on the stage image, and the audience is treated to as much surprise as can be elicited under the circumstance. If there is no music the lighting person makes a sound or says, "Open eyes!".

Assignment: Solos as duets. Photo by Jeffrey Huereque

As the piece unfolds, the two players divide their focus between the piece they prepared and the one performed by the partner. They must remain centered in their conceptual creation and simultaneously project an image of stage unity no matter how seemingly contrasting the two pieces are.

Since our vision and brains create the perceived unity of the stage picture, there is already a strong tendency for the audience to take in the duet as a single piece with two performers, rather than two pieces with a soloist each. But the wonder is that so often, the theatrical questions posed by one player are answered by the other, quite instinctively. Movements, gesture, use of space, begin to gel or to complement one another. The themes intermesh. The ending satisfies our expectation for completion and closure. And all this may be taking place on a very abstract level, and brought about unconsciously rather than deliberately. When that happens, the result is magical, and again, we can say: "The Genie is here!"

There are so many things to attend to in this exercise: for one, the question of sound. If *both* performers had planned to have music or sound and both gave cues and directions to the tech person, the tech person has the work cut out for either him or her! For one thing, there must be two CD players with a mixer that can bring out each music together or separately. That way, interesting blends can happen, in this exercise as well as others. The mixer should have enough channels to accommodate music and a microphone. Its manipulation is a question of focus. When the focus on stage shifts from one player to the other, the sound goes with it. So the players on stage must be very aware of where the focus is, and learn how to "give, or take, focus". There are many ways that this can be done. For instance one can reduce his or her own importance by slowing down, by repetition of motion as in a "perpetual mobile", by freezing, making eye focus aimed on the other person, or using his/her body to "point" toward the other, in a way that doesn't seem to involve persona or the story. It is simply a sculptural and compositional element. When a performer is totally involved with his or her piece, it's difficult to do but must be attempted. In "real life", it's like being able to listen to the other person's argument when there is a disagreement. Not always easy. If the two must use the same space at any time, it can be an interesting problem, usually solved by mirroring, or shadowing. I've had two people sit on the same chair, one on the other's lap, seemingly oblivious of the spatial double use! But other solutions can be found on the wing, so to speak. It's always interesting to see how this assignment works, in so many different ways, and how even the color scheme may be totally harmonious, by chance!

Because the crutch of words is either minimal or non-existent, everything else on stage—performers, light, sound, objects, etc., must be expressive, both as concept and work of art. This means that, in parallel efforts, one must create a meaningful piece that has something to say that the player strongly wishes to say, as well as having a form and structure that will place it in the category of work of art rather than a didactic statement.

I notice that I often use the word "art" in this book. I realize that the word has undergone many metamorphoses in the past century, with some artists attempting to obscure and erase the boundaries between art and "life", or "everyday life". Some conceptual artists state their artistic intent in text instead of doing it. Others design but leave the actual making of the artwork to others, usually professional construction workers or painters.

To conjure "art" as often as I do might seem old fashioned to some. In some circles the word has taken on a negative connotation. All of this is academic, in my view. Whatever name one wishes to give it, I believe that "art" is a very recognizable entity, both as thing and as activity. The rest is cant. Sorry about that. Happenings were art. Actions were art. Body art was art. The fact of doing something that has no place in the daily continuum of our lives in a utilitarian way is art. So, OK. Now that this is clarified, I continue.

Participating in DbD requires a leap of the imagination, and an availability that seizes the moment with all it has to offer, ready and able to use chance as well as choices, and concepts that have been brewing in our thoughts and feelings, pushing to emerge. This emergence becomes an amalgam between idea and form, as all good art does, plus the secret ingredients of immediacy and surprise. The costumes, assembled from bits and pieces of clothing or objects, things used in unexpected ways—bags as hats, skirts as wigs, masks as breasts, manikin feet as hands, etc.—seem to herald things to come in mysterious ways. They become glyphs for signals and meanings, even before anything happens. After "Eyes Out", when the piece begins with its strange set, its painterly lights, unexpected soundtrack, we are primed to participate in what seems like a community ritual, a feast for the senses and the mind that turns viewing into participation. We "tell ourselves the story" as it unfolds, each member of the audience concocting a different tale. The set uses the space in such ways as to transform the studio, giving it a different locale and atmosphere with each piece. Sometimes immense, deserted, or claustrophobic; rococo or gothic; low on the ground, or hanging high from the rafters; sets are created with simple boxes, open screens, chairs, *shmattes*, ropes, able to transmogrify themselves at will, All the wooden pieces are painted white. The gelled lights cast colored shadow images on the white upstage wall. Three flats on wheels, one white and two black, can be placed in a way as to transform the space. We have a large amount of props. I myself don't even know the half of what we store. People bring strange objects all the time, or old things that have outlived their welcome in homes. They get a new life in the theater space, most often as other than what they were meant to be originally, in a surreal reincarnation reminiscent of Giorgio de Chirico or Salvador Dalí. There is color, black, white, gold, shimmering things, glitter, sequins, artificial plants and flowers, circus costumes, old army gear and fatigues, tiaras, bridal gowns, samovars, wheelchairs, masks of animals and demons, *Commedia* masks, folding chairs, tables on wheels, kitchen utensils, guns, and so on. The Music Booth contains instruments that are classical, and sound or noise-makers that are improvised. There are old wood and glass laundry boards, tubes that sing, stones that drum. There are flutes, Jew's harps, xylophones, zithers, bells, toy pianos, Chinese gongs. Every combination of sounds is available and is used. I like both the "right" CD that is chosen also by chance most of the time, and the live combo that becomes another player in the theater experience.

When a piece begins, we are witnessing what could be assumed to be the inside of a person's mind, its dreams, its memories, its subconscious life, its deepest origins and its futuristic projections. Also its hidden desires, sometimes sadistic, sometimes erotic. It is always fascinating, but when it is also supported by a strong formal composition, when it becomes a work of art, it is doubly enthralling. I never tire of watching such work. I am always amazed at the images my students come up with, and the total involvement it represents. Doing by Doing then becomes tangible to the performers, something they can take home, transform, transmute

Music Table. Photo by Rachel Rosenthal

into other art forms or activities if they wish, but always buoyed by an energy motor and a style that affords endless inventions and opulent results.

TECHNIQUES

Depending on time, I bring in the technique exercises in late afternoon, early evening, or leave them for the next day. Here are some.

Single Images

If there are twelve students, I separate them into four groups of three. They stand on stage, facing the audience. Members of the audience volunteer, and for each group, one person will get up and whisper the same adjective in each player's ear. The exercise consists in taking the adjective and becoming its essence. So you don't play a person who is "*sad*", for instance, you play the "*essence of sadness*", or "*sadness itself*". The thing to watch for, as we choose the adjective, is that it's

Images. Photo by Kate Noonan

not something that needs an object to be expressed, such as "*envious*". When the lights come on, after the obligatory blackout, all three players embody the adjective. It has to permeate every part of their body and voice, from tip to toe. The exercise lasts approximately a minute and a half, during which each player pushes the whole-body expression as far as they can, creating what amounts to a caricature or an icon. When they have reached maximum expression, we black them out. Every group of three repeats the exercise with different adjectives. With the feedback, the audience tries to guess the adjective. If they do, it shows the exercise was successful, and if they don't, the students who have just performed it become aware of their failure to clearly communicate.

Double Images

Again, four threesomes. This time, two volunteers whisper one adjective each in the student's ears. As a result each student has two adjectives to work with. If the second adjective happens by chance to be the antithesis of the first, seemingly negating it, think twice before asking for an alternative adjective because sometimes these poles-apart contradictions are close to some people's personalities, the two attributes living within the same individual. People are living contradictions! As the three students absorb the meaning of their two adjectives, the job is to fuse them. It is not a question of being able to portray the two adjectives alternatively, but simultaneously! Which means that one must distribute the two within the instrument in such a way as to display each in different parts of the body. As an example, "benign" and "inebriated". One may be "benign" in face and voice expression, and "inebriated" in the body motion. There are infinite possibilities. It's a very fun exercise, and the "charades" aspect brings levity to the group. However, it is also a very important exercise, one that prepares the building of a persona. If the Double Image can be found for a character, it becomes its core, with layers added as the character becomes more complex.

BIOYA Redux

Somewhere in the early evening, we create a new BIOYA. These wonderful group pieces open people up in many important ways. They have a certain dynamic that allows students to go beyond the rigor of an exercise, and that propels them fully

into the artistic inventiveness and flow that they are capable of and that they sometimes fail to access in the exercises. It gives a chance for performers to connect creatively with many people within a piece. This happens in ways that are productive for people because they have experienced the students' various personalities in the previous processes and have developed a common vocabulary in class that they can draw on spontaneously. This permits them to trust the other on levels they are capable of attaining and sustaining. They are enabled to boldly explore areas they had never tackled before, one reason being that the BIOYA is a group piece and, as such, it takes away the individual's anxiety of being singly responsible for the success of the improvisation as a whole. Responsibility becomes a communal affair. They use costuming to bring out the characteristics of what they are portraying. They use the set, and learn how to play the stage for maximum expressiveness. Moreover, they have lost their timidity, their self-centeredness, their competitiveness, their awkwardness, their narcissism, simply by the fact of focusing only on the work of art that is being developed collectively and with devotion. The lavish use of "Units" facilitates choreography and composition, making it reasonably easy to attain form. The fact of wanting to make good art first and foremost has the magical consequence of sweeping away much mud from our beleaguered psyches! So the BIOYAs, if properly paced, can become barometers of progress and achievement, different perhaps for each individual, but very palpable nevertheless in the group as a whole. When a BIOYA is successful, I compliment profusely and am very enthused. The players glow and are happy. They have experienced good theater and become far more confident in their work as a whole.

The next exercise is a hard one, because it's a solo and needs time. It's late in the day, people are pretty tired by now, and that factor is necessary for the exercise to work.

Object Exercise: "One Person, One Object, One Emotion"

The students are sitting in a line against the audience-side wall, and take their turn in whatever order we start, left to right, or right to left. One by one, they will each do the exercise. I announce that this is the only exercise of the weekend that is

"Object Exercise". Photo by Kate Noonan

designed to be only for them, not for the audience. i.e. it is *not* a performance. They are not obliged to entertain, or even to make art.

One of the Slaves of Love does the lights. There is no set, no costume, and no music. The student stands facing the upstage wall. A wide spotlight is aimed at center stage. The student relaxes and empties the mind as much as possible. I go to the Props and Costumes Room and choose an object. Sometimes I combine objects to create an assemblage. Sometimes there are several objects of the same kind (several flowers, *shmattes*, or road blocks, for instance). Sometimes I put together a couple of objects to enhance their effect (a manikin head inside a bird cage, for example), and ask the students to behave toward the objects as if they were a single one. My choices are totally instinctive. I see the person, get a feeling of who they are, and enter the Props Room without thinking, in a slight trance. I scan the props all around me, and usually an object or a combination of objects will offer itself. I take them without question.

After having chosen the object I return to the studio and deposit it on the floor, in the pool of light. I make the necessary adjustments, and then I go back to my place noisily, so as to indicate to the person with their face to the wall that they can turn around.

I've asked the student to "see" the object, and do nothing. The first sight tells them what the object is, and what it's used for. Is it a knife? A rope? A target made of colored *shmattes*? A pail of garbage? A gas mask? Sometimes the object is abstract and difficult to "read"; sometimes it's an obvious cliché. The student is to wait, contemplating the object, until the surface identity disappears, and the actual "object" reveals itself and triggers an emotion.

I tell the students that when they feel an emotion emerging, they should "pressure-cook" it before taking action, in order to intensify the feeling. At the point that they sense that they have done that, they should *react first with the voice*. (If they don't, it becomes progressively harder to bring the sound out.) Let the voice lead, and then let the response to the object take whatever form and whatever time it must. The object can be apprehended for itself, be a trigger for a memory, remind the student of another object, or introduce a whole event that it has become a metaphor or symbol for, as when a young man in one of my early DbDs sang the whole *Kaddish* to a black coat!

As the students take time, doing nothing but gazing at the object, every person in the audience is actually doing the exercise along with them. They too gaze at the object, with their own response to it, wondering what the person will finally do, and judging whether I chose the right object or not. I watch closely and wait. I can tell whether the person is waiting long enough, or getting nervous about taking too long and then faking it. If one continues to wait beyond the moment of truth, the effect fritters away. If one goes too soon, the deep feeling hasn't emerged, and the exercise is botched. It is also an exercise in knowing when to release.

Note: Sometimes a performer will retain an impulse and then attempts to release it beyond the moment of its existence. Eugen Herrigel deals beautifully with the question of right release time in *Zen in the Art of Archery*.

When the exercise is done right, the student may touch and handle the object, sometimes altering it, according to the psychic impulse culminating the exercise.

The climactic action may take several seconds or several minutes. It may bring screams, tears, song, one word, hysterical laughter, a physical event, whatever is appropriate. It can involve the object physically, sometimes violently, sometimes lovingly. It may bring mirth, or a totally unexpected activity. One may never touch the object, or may kick it, or cradle it, or transform it, or ignore it. Any reaction is acceptable, so long as the exercise was done correctly, with the often long wait for the right moment.

It is also important to take the reaction to its completion and not to segue into a new emotion that may develop. The exercise is for a single emotion.

I don't give feedback unless the exercise was not done right: too quickly, too theatrically, and not authentically. Sometimes the student is stuck. Nothing comes. They go back to their seat, empty. I don't say or do much. Let it sink in. Sometimes I hug the people who have been visibly very affected. I often have to put out paper tissues, if people get into a crying mode. We may talk about it or not. I warn people that whatever happened will be meaningful for them, at one time or another.

Sometimes, after all the exercises are done, I ask the group who among them felt they got the "right" object, and most of the time they all do. Sometimes a person will feel that the object was "wrong". Oddly enough, those are usually the objects that I felt were "perfect" and chose perhaps too intellectually! Often, a "perfect object" will be too intense for the person who will reject it unconsciously.

Some students have experienced instant breakthroughs of a spectacular sort. Others take longer to feel its consequence. It is a completely individual process and, most often, the aspect it takes on stage is seemingly tame compared with its ultimate effect on the performer. I had a young man as a student, who had a very conventional theater background, learned in a dramatic academy. His expression never went further down than his chin. His body was stiff and lackluster. I gave him a mound of white cotton rope, the kind that is sewn in the bottom of costumes to make a roll. After a long time, he picked up strands of the rope and beat the walls with it with growing violence and fury. He beat, and beat, for minutes! He continued to study with me after that. He was a changed man and performer. His whole body was expressive, and he became a wonderful physical comedian and the main performer in my Instant Theatre.

BIOYA again

After the "Object Exercise", a BIOYA is definitely in order, no matter how late it is, and how tired we are! The Object Exercise has shifted the level of the weekend, and the people have entered into a different area. There is a need for openness, relaxation, sincerity, connection, and, above all, return to art-making, but perhaps with a different attitude, and a sense of having experienced a meaningful and very intimate event. The group improvisation takes on a deeper expression, there is closer attention to form and content, and the work is usually of a caliber that leaves the participants with a high that carries into Sunday, and gives the work a glow.

Sunday: "Power"

Again, the people return for the 9:30 am session, but the Slaves of Love have been there since 9 am, cleaning up, setting up, starting the coffee, etc. There is a nice atmosphere of anticipation. People are sharing their experience, some slept well, some had strange dreams, some couldn't sleep. I am a stickler for punctuality, and don't take well to lateness. Whenever necessary I lecture my students about that, explaining that theater, whether it be live, film, television, radio, or any work in the entertainment industry, is based on time. To be late is a cause for being fired. But, more importantly, I believe that because we live such short lives, time is precious. Anything you care to say about the importance of time and respect for it is good and important. Nothing is worse than a *waste* of time.

Circle Talk: "Power"

We sit in a circle again, and I improvise my Power speech.

> The people who come to a workshop such as mine are artists and would-be artists. Whatever the case, they are here because something in them has ventured from the beaten path and onto the pebble-strewn road. There is a fairy tale that talks of a "hero" who goes on a quest. His first test is coming to a fork in the road. The road on the right is nicely paved, smooth, and straight. The one on the left is covered with pebbles and sharp stones, winds up and down mountains, and curls around boulders. The hero ponders and then chooses the pebble road on the left. Things are stark and difficult, but his resolve is strong and eventually he is able to vanquish all dragons and monsters in his way, grab the boon (a treasure, a magic object, a princess) and race with it

back to society. The "bad brothers" who chose the easy road on the right are lured to a tavern on the way, drink themselves into a stupor, and miss out on the adventure and the treasure. Such is the metaphor for the life of the artist. It's the hard road, and it's the boon. *And* the return to society!

So I like to consider that all my students are artists, and that they are drawn to the hard road. They may never be rich, but the boon they bring back is of another nature entirely, and far more precious than money. I like to think of that boon as being what I call Power with a capital P, as opposed to power with a small p. The small-p power is the one that has a bad rep. It is ego power-over, power-against, power that uses and abuses, power that links us to the destructive aspect of Earth and Nature. Power with a capital P is the energy one gathers from the Earth itself, that empowers us to create, thereby connecting us with the creative, rather than Nature's destructive field.

When we are able to pull that Power into ourselves, we become what we aspire to be. We are able to bring forth objects or actions that are heroic by definition, and sometimes remarkable. The true heroes of society are those who have brought forth the inventions, discoveries, new forms, beneficial human works and relationships that have advanced our lives and our ability to understand and connect with Nature as a whole. Those persons are visionaries who can tell the difference between works that are valuable to the whole Planet as well as to its human inhabitants, and those works that enrich human beings momentarily at the expense of other beings and of the Planet in its entirety. It is a very fine line and a hard realization to come by. It is so easy to feel good without thought of others, be they people or ecosystems, for instance. Or whales. Or foreign cultures. It is hard to separate our hubris from our accomplishments. It is hard to make art when wondering "What for?" "For who?" It is hard to keep going if our work is misunderstood and denigrated, as has been the case time and again with artists who were true innovators ahead of their time. These people, whose works are now so highly prized and priced, are the ones who stuck to the pebble road in spite of the blisters. They are the true heroes. That is one aspect of the pebble road. There are others. How to tell which road when a wonderful result comes from a twisted and flawed action? How to tell the difference between political compliments and sincere acclaim? How to recognize honesty or how to choose between two lesser evils?

I do believe that artists are people with a sense of responsibility, simply by the fact of having dedicated their lives to creation. That responsibility begins with their own person. I believe that artists are conduits for the inventiveness of Nature, of the Cosmos; that artists, in a modest way, are human incarnations of the Power of the Universe. Just as athletes should feel responsible for the health and strength of their bodies as the instrument through which their talent flows, so do artists have the responsibility of keeping themselves healthy, strong and clear, in order to be able to transmit to the world the visions of their life adventure in art. Sadly, many artists don't see it that way. They feel the sting of being disrespected and rejected by society, or accepted and adulated for all the wrong reasons, and may fall into despair. This despair brings on palliatives that are in themselves destructive and vicious. Many artists drink, take drugs, and abuse themselves and others. I feel for their pain and understand it. It is very hard being a person who brings forth something from nothing. Who among us doesn't fear the blank page or canvas, the block? Who doesn't fear being or becoming a sorcerer's apprentice? Or who does fear those things and continues anyway? Simply putting out what is in us doesn't necessarily make it good. The angel and the devil must fight it out, sometimes to exhaustive and exhausting ends. Has any non-artist ever understood the artist's angst? The constant quest to attain a perfection that is unattainable? Such is the artist's fate. A torture of Tantalus!

I don't consider myself a philosopher or a seer. I am an artist who gives space and time to other artists to allow us to walk the pebble road our own way and bring back whatever boon is destined to be ours.

When I look at the faces in the circle, I see hope, fear, and expectation. They hope for answers and an "Open Sesame!" to the grotto of wonders. I tell another fairy tale: the hero is a child who lives with his or her parents in a hut at the edge of the forest. Life is simple, predictable, no surprises. One day, the hero hears "the Call". It can come in various forms: an old person, a little person, an animal, a golden ball that starts to roll . . . The child follows the invitation, answers the Call. It takes him or her into the rabbit hole, or deep into the scary forest, filled with dangers. But eventually the answer comes; the boon is discovered and brought back. The trick is to *Answer the Call*. Many of us get that Call at some time in our life, and ignore it. That is a bad mistake. I have experienced that tragic error and had to pay for it. Whatever was to be mine in understanding and accomplishment became elusive and faded away. It took me many decades of hard work to recapture it, and not in its initial clarity and thrill. Not answering the Call may also be dangerous, and engender neuroses, accidents, and defeats. The access to Earth Power is the panacea. However, it must be used judiciously. Spread it around! Be not Power-full, but Power-flowing! And don't show off or brag! Especially not with family or friends. You are shifting levels, and metamorphosing into a new being. It is heady stuff, but very scary for those who liked you comfy and just as you were. You may have to hide your light under a bushel when you are with people who can't follow your path. It's the humane thing to do, unless you find yourself obliged to drop some people from your life. That may be painful but necessary. You will know when it is happening. Just pay attention, be awake and aware, and don't succumb to pity or denial. Each of us has lessons to learn, one way or another, those who soar as well as those who drop by the wayside.

Star Meditation

After the Power talk, I place the twelve people in a circle on the floor in the middle of the room, lying on their backs with their heads in the center of the circle, their arms at their sides, in star formation. As I speak, I move around the formation, taking a step with each new image. I keep circling until the end of the meditation.

First, I tell them that they are lying on the ground, the soil is moist and takes the contour of their body, that it becomes a template for their form. I have them breathe, and suggest relaxation images starting at the top of their heads, going down. With closed eyes, I have them check every part of their bodies for any tension or knots,

"Star Meditation", 1980. Photo by Mary Collins

and tell them to "shed their macramé suits". The checking descends from the top of the skull gradually down to the feet and the toes.

When the toes have been reached and relaxed, I improvise this meditation:

> Imagine that your toes are planted in the center of Earth's core. (The music begins at this point—I use good world music for this, perhaps an Indian Raga.) That's where we believe the hardest and heaviest metals have sunk: iron ore, perhaps crystalline, perhaps a huge diamond. It is the center of Power, the atomic oven, the motor of the Planet. Its heart.
>
> Rise into the foot, inside the outer core, rotating against the direction of the Earth's rotation, creating a strong magnetic field, a furnace, like a huge peach stone in the center of the Earth, generating intense heat, Power, and the identity of our planetary Mother.
>
> When you rise up to your calves, you are in the mantle, the molten, viscous planetary flesh between the core and the rock lithosphere where the tectonic plates move, and the continents ride.
>
> You rise into the knees with the convection currents of the mantle that carry you further up, where the molten lava erupts through cracks in the plates and the crust, to give birth to new Earth flesh, in the depth of the ocean and on the surface of the Planet.
>
> When you reach the thighs, you are just under the plates, conveyer belts of continents across the globe, tearing, colliding them, and creating the geography we know today. As you move with the plates, you emerge deep into the ocean beds, matrices of life, and become acquainted with the very first expressions of that life, the simple organisms at the bottom of the sea. There, you witness the invention of the food chain, sex and death. The organisms evolve, adapting to circumstance and environment, becoming more complex and taking more fantastic shapes as you rise up your legs, and come closer to the ocean surface.
>
> There, sea and crust meet, animals are half-fish half-terrestrials, as you reach your genitals and pelvis, and become aware of the enormous metamorphosis experienced by the plants and animals whose lifelines had to transform the poisonous oxygen and to accept existing in air instead of water.
>
> You rise into your stomach, and there, you have crossed into land. You marvel at the diversity of living things, in and on the soil, in water, in the air, the range of sizes from the micro to the macro of existence, and the role that each plays in the orchestra of life.
>
> As you rise into your solar plexus, you begin to climb up the mountains of the crust, and are surrounded with weather, those huge, global cycling motions

of water and atmosphere, that bring life or death on Earth. There are birds, and human-made machines that fly as well.

You are now in your chest and keep going up, reaching areas where air is thin. The sun is bright above the clouds, but unable to warm the sea of gases, which is cooling fast. Some gases trap the heat, creating havoc on Earth.

You are up in your shoulders and, looking back, you see the line that separates the blue from the black and the moving line of day and night on Earth. Behind you are the blue and white whirls of weather, including the dangerous eye, hovering still, within the spiraling tentacles of the hurricane. Above you, there is a canopy of stars, including our star the Sun, burning bright in a sea of blackness.

When you reach your neck, you are escaping the pull of the Earth, and are able to approach our satellite the Moon, circling it to view its dark side, and to be catapulted still further into the silence of space.

As you come to your mouth, you are voyaging within the Solar System, experiencing the waves of solar wind, the lessening of gravity from Earth, and you pass our family of bodies that also circle our star: Mars, Jupiter, Saturn, Uranus, Pluto, with all their satellites, and the space debris large enough to have names, even if only as numbers.

When you arrive at your nose, you escape from the Solar System, and fly into the immensity of our galaxy the Milky Way, pulling back to recognize its form, its spiraling arms, noticing the activity of the voracious Black Hole at its center, and further back yet, to view the several other galaxies that are our sisters in the cluster to which we belong.

You are now in your eyes. You are able to discern the structure of the Universe in which we live, its shape, its infinity, its mysteries, and its inhabiting objects. You see galaxies, nebulae, stars born and dying, some in throes, some in immense explosions. You see quasars, pulsars, and white dwarfs; you see sights that occurred shortly after the Big Bang.

When in your forehead, all the atoms of your body disembody. They scatter and enter the race away from each other, the great Entropy. And as your atoms dash through the Universe, they encounter trillions of trillions of other atoms, also dashing away from each other, and they recognize the atoms that formed the bodies around this star formation on this floor.

You are now beyond form, shape, and objects. Infinitesimally tiny lines sing. You are in the "music of the spheres", the music-making "strings". Perhaps the basic stuff! Your brain is able to imagine all these things, and use them for meditation, for science, for art. And so you gather yourself from all parts of the Universe that you just traveled, and reconstitute your body and your individuality.

You return to your place on this floor. But you are always connected to the Universe, the Cosmos, and to our Mother, the Planet Earth.

And so place your arms so the palms of your hands face the space around you, turned upward, to capture the waves that pass between and around you. Now raise your arms so that your hands, palms, and fingers act like lightning rods, catching those waves, and fill yourselves with their Power. Now raise your arms above your head so that your hands encounter all the other hands in the center of the star formation, and touch as many hands as possible to share in and amplify this capture.

Note: The above meditation is an approximation of what I say, since it is improvised and, therefore, always a little different. I leave to the reader who wishes to use this exercise the choice of whether to include material pertaining to global warming, or not. It would probably depend on context, who the group of participants represent, what their focus is. I haven't done it yet but am considering using that material as our climate change becomes more drastic. I also advise whoever wishes to use this material to acquaint themselves with the latest theories and discoveries pertaining to the Cosmos. Our understanding of it is constantly changing.

The students take a few minutes to come back to the moment and the place while touching fingers and hands above their heads, eyes closed.

Power Movement

This is a good time to have the group move, connected, in slow and difficult groupings, with extreme balances and partnering. It shouldn't take too long as it is followed by a long exercise.

Climbing the Mountain

I tell the students that, in the next exercise, they will be climbing a mountain. But instead of doing so vertically, they will do it horizontally, transforming the plane of the floor from a flat ground to a soaring mountain, very steep, and all of one rock,

"Climbing the Mountain". Photo by Rachel Rosenthal

such as El Capitan in Yosemite Valley. The group will start to "climb" from one side of the studio space to the other, the long way. They get ready by lying face down on the floor, and climb three abreast. I tell them that they must be as realistic as possible, to visualize their ascent in all its details, through their senses: the cold wind, the rough rock, the little bushes growing out of cracks, the birds flying by. If they haven't experienced mountain climbing themselves, they must try to remember the movies in which they viewed it: the fingers, the toes, the pitons hammered into the rock, the ropes. Keep glancing down at the receding valley floor, and up at the diminishing height. When they arrive at the summit, I have them wait silently for everyone to finish their climb. It isn't a race, and each person does it at their own pace. I ask them not to help each other up because they must individually experience the effort and the accomplishment. When everyone is up, there is usually a moment of euphoria and hilarity, when a sense of the absurdity of it all sinks in, after the tremendous effort, sweat and all, that went into the "climb"!

I do this exercise to extremely dramatic and appropriate music (*Utrenja* by Penderecki), that echoes perfectly the danger, anxiety, and triumph of the action. At this point, approximately 15 minutes in, the music becomes a quasi-religious chorale and I begin to speak over it into a hand-held microphone. I say:

> You have now reached the top of the mountain. You are on a high plateau. Imagine that, without turning, you now face, not the drop of the mountain

"A Place of Power". Photographer unknown

you have just climbed, but a large meadow, high on the top of the rock. You decide to explore this plateau.

The sun is bright, but the air is cold. Under your feet the grass is sharp and green, there are outcroppings and boulders protruding from the field. There are some flowers. An eagle passes overhead! You hear the sound of a waterfall nearby.

As you explore, you suddenly realize this is an ancient place of Power. You find your own place of Power and own it. Fill yourselves with that Power. There is plenty where that came from! When you are full, begin to radiate it, like the Sun!

You find yourself making the sound of Power.

Little by little, they raise their voices, louder and louder, using their breaths to the fullest, and exuding Power as they do. The sounds emerge from their throats, soft at first, gradually gaining in volume.

Distribute your Power as a gift to the world!

They focus their movement and their voices outward, turning to reach all directions.

Be specific in your giving!

They begin to direct their donations toward other members of the group. The individuals give and take, sharing Power, usually in pairs at first, touching each other and looking into each other's eyes. At this point, the group begins to act spontaneously and together. I've seen them form circles, hold hands, create smaller groups, sit, stand, chant in harmonious chorales, lift each other up in the air, and/or make a Power formation to send a collective force up into the atmosphere and back down to Earth. By the time they begin to act on their own, continuing the vocal output, I stop the music, which has become inaudible anyway, and let whatever happens happen. The lights have been steadily brightening throughout this process. Like a rising midday Sun. When I feel the energy of the group has been spent, I have them lie down, relax and breathe. The lights go low, or out. The students need a rest.

Lunch break

After a while, I call a break, which is usually the lunch break. The lunch breaks Saturday and Sunday vary as to time, according to how long the morning processes have taken. Lunches usually last 45 minutes to an hour, either brown bag or in a neighborhood restaurant.

The above three processes on Sunday morning are crucial to the emotional curve of the weekend. Up to now, there were very personal moments, especially in the "Voice Circle" and the "Object Exercise". But the majority of exercises were techniques designed to enable the group to make good art within the shortest time imaginable. But in the Sunday morning exercises, I attempt to move the psyches from the human to the cosmic and integrate the two. "Climbing the Mountain" amalgamates body and spirit, joining together each individual's physical and emotional selves. For the first half of the day on Sunday, the order in which the processes are experienced is very important, and, in my opinion, cannot be moved around without losing their full impact on the person and the group.

The written description of the Sunday Power exercises may seem childish. They read that way to me. Like children's games. However, the same thing performed in all seriousness not only is not childish, but also has the inherent capacity to transform, and to achieve remarkable growth in individuals. I believe it is the combination of vivid imagery along with total body enactment and expression that provides the needed chemistry for the cumulative effect of the weekend to click and fuse. It is not unusual to find people crying, laughing, hugging, and going through states that seem new and exhilarating to them.

After the break are more techniques and art making, and a solo improv that can clarify and fix the work and provide psychological benefit for the students in a way that can take them one step further, both in their art and in their lives.

Before getting back to the techniques, we do a number of free improvs, in full regalia of sets, costumes, live music, lights, and performance, with varied amounts of people in the casts. Some are duos, some have three or more, and always a great BIOYA to start and/or end with. By now I feel I can vary the order and the content of the Sunday pieces, both according to the needs of the group, and to keep myself from being bored by too rigid a program.

"Bringing the Power down to Earth". Photo by Helena Ruffin

PROCESSES AND FORMS

There is usually time for just two different exercises after the improvs. The following exercises are some of the ones I choose from: in the next two exercises, I allow 30 words maximum if students need language for their concept.

Life Stories Solos: "The Story of Your Life in Three Minutes"

I give five minutes for the students to decide what to do. The piece is mostly successful if metaphoric and abstract, finding the essence of the life curve and playing it out. This forces a symbolic approach to one's existence, and a quick assessment and understanding of it. Sometimes it triggers enough enlightenment for change to eventually occur, if need be.

Hidden Aspects Solos

I give four minutes for people to think of an aspect of their person that they don't want the world to see. One by one, they present this part of themselves, as a three-minute solo piece, with the props and costume they deem necessary for the theme. The lights are improvised, and again, the performer may give certain indications to the tech people if they need it. Usually, these pieces are done simply and without much visual enhancing. The aspects in question can be either positive or negative. They range from bad habits, things contrary to the image they wish to project, to real problems of an emotional nature. These exercises are sometimes cathartic and help the student move on, if the aspect has the nature of a block.

Brief Encounters

I took the title and idea from the British film of 1945. In the movie, the two protagonists meet by chance in a railway station. They meet again and again. Eventually they are in love. Both are married with attachments, and they must part definitively. In the exercise, two people start at opposite sides of the stage, and they meet in the middle, and part, over and over. Their meetings become progressively more intimate and urgent. At the last meeting, they part forever. This exercise is wordless, and must express the progressive seriousness of their relationship through the body.

It may be a love situation, or any other emotional expression. The importance of the exercise is the feelings underlying it, and the gradual transformation of the attachment, showing how their relationship intensifies through their behavior and actions.

"Thaïs", 1980. Photo by Rachel Rosenthal

Thaïs

I tell the "story", taken from a novel by the twentieth-century French writer Anatole France. In the early Christian days, in the Middle East, there lived a very rich and successful courtesan called Thaïs, and a monk called Paphnutius. Thaïs represents sin, and Paphnutius, who spends his time mortifying his flesh and doing penance, is a saint. They meet, she laughs at him, and he becomes obsessed with needing to convert her and saving her soul. They meet several times throughout the book, and each time, there is a subtle change. Thaïs becomes more virtuous, and Paphnutius more depraved. To make a long story short, it ends with Thaïs entering a convent, and Paphnutius breaking into her cell and raping her! Again, the two performers start at opposite sides of the stage and establish their characters briefly. There are several encounters, each one showing the subtle change they bring upon each other. Finally they part and exit at opposite sides, having become, she, virtuous, he, sinful. The trick is to remain in character rather than taking on a completely new persona.

We are now ready for the . . .

RAMBLER

This is really a glorified BIOYA. It simply is longer, uses some words, and utilizes as many of the DbD techniques as the piece seems to require. Ramblers usually start with one person who somehow sets the theme, either verbally, visually, aurally, or any combination thereof. Because it can last anywhere between 15 and 45 minutes, it has high latitude in its composition. The person on lights can divide it into sections by creating two blackouts, say, for three sections (the performers must be told in advance so as not to think the piece is ending), or keep going but with very varied moods and coloring, perhaps inspired by changes in music (canned or live, or both), or in the playing itself. No two Ramblers are alike, of course. But it's important that the performers be *very* aware of how the piece begins and be ready to enhance and support its initial style and motif statement. The theme must be kept in mind and developed, or transformed if there is a metaphor to be discovered and played out. These Ramblers, only one of which is experienced in the DbD, are really the crowning glory of my training. I love Ramblers. I am always surprised and amazed by the endless variety of their look, themes, styles, and productions. What delight it is to see the result of all our work, in a piece that is substantial and theatrically mature. And to think that it is only done once and viewed by so few people! A hefty dose of Zen helps us swallow that fact!

Final Circle

Well, it is Sunday just before midnight. We are all played out. Just one more thing to do, an important thing, for it bonds us, terminates the weekend on a high note, gives closure to our emotional journey, reveals the hidden meaning of DbD, and sends us back to our individual lives with joy, hope, satisfaction, new friends and colleagues, and especially, a new theatrical language that we have all learned to speak together (so to speak!), and can use in as many ways as there are individual DbD alumni willing to keep the torch lit and the fire burning.

We sit in a circle for the last time, but this time, carrying one or several percussion instruments. Some have drums, others gongs, bells, rattles and other sound-makers including keyboards and flutes. I thank all the students, I thank the Slaves of Love, and then I tell The Dibidi Story.

The Dibidi Story

It's time now to tell the true meaning of DbD. As you know, the exoteric meaning is Doing by Doing, which is the basis of my philosophy and training method. But there is an esoteric meaning that only those who have taken DbD are aware of.

In 1954, I lived in a loft in New York's Lower Manhattan, in a very run-down district that no longer exists, in a condemned building that was going to be destroyed. My posse at the time consisted of Merce Cunningham, John Cage, Bob Rauschenberg, Jasper Johns, Cy Twombly, and their whole entourage. One day, Earle Brown, Carolyn Brown's composer husband (Carolyn was Merce's star dancer), told me his cat had a litter and that he would give me one of the kittens. I came and chose a female who had a very peculiar look in her eyes, and I called her Dibidi. At the time, I also had a boy cat named Tioutik, given to me by Ray Johnson, the artist. Dibidi was supposed to become Tioutik's girlfriend, however they never connected on that level, but rather platonically as siblings.

In the summer of 1955, my father died in Beverly Hills, California, when on vacation. I flew over for the funeral and left my cats to be cared for by a friend. When I returned after two weeks, Dibidi was missing. I was completely devastated and searched for her far and wide, in the neighborhood and the whole little building, with no success. I was especially upset because the cats used to go up the fire escape onto the roof to play and relieve themselves, and there were a number of chimneys there, some of which had been bricked over while I was away.

I didn't dare to think that she could have fallen into one of those and be buried alive! After three days and nights, I was on the roof, leaning over the rim of one of the chimneys and weeping. I cried for my father, and I cried for

Dibidi. Photo by Rachel Rosenthal

Dibidi and Tioutik on the fire escape on Pearl Street. Photo by Rachel Rosenthal

Dibidi. As I watched my tears falling down into the black shaft, I suddenly saw a tiny almond-shaped green light, deep down inside it. And then another. She was looking up at me. I quickly dried my eyes so I could see better and calculated that she was probably at the height of the second floor in the building. My loft was on the fifth floor. I spoke French to her, as always, and called her name. She let out a weak and cavernous meow. I told her to hang on and that I would get her out. Bob and Jap (Rauschenberg and Johns) were not home, it was Saturday afternoon and they had probably gone to the movies. I tried calling the Society for the Prevention of Cruelty to Animals (SPCA), but no one answered. I called the Police, who came and laughed at me. I threw them out. I took some tools, broke into the print shop on the second floor and started to hammer through the bricks that had walled up their fireplace. Every so often I would run up the stairs onto the roof to yell down to Dibidi not to give up, that I was coming. It took me five hours to make a hole big enough to put my head and an arm through. I had miscalculated by about five feet. She was covered with plaster dust from my digging. I saw that she was hanging on by her claws to an incline that became a vertical shaft above her head. I had to get her out while she still had strength enough to hang on. I tried to make a little elevator, a cardboard platform held up by ropes. I lowered it but soon realized she was afraid of letting go. I knew I had to get her up by a noose around her neck. I vaguely remembered learning that cats didn't easily die by hanging. But I had never made a noose, let alone one for my cat.

I tried calling SPCA again, without success. So I prayed that I would be successful on the first try, made a noose and, after some effort, got her by the neck and pulled. She was out and in my arms! I don't even remember how! I ran upstairs with her to give her milk and food. But starved and thirsty as she was, she only accepted to eat and drink after she had thanked me profusely, head on the floor, backside up in the air, making the loudest purring sound ever! She was so weak that she kept falling over, but kept it up. Her claws were worn to the quick and bleeding. I cleaned her up and never let her out of my sight. Dibidi and I had a special relationship after that. It was a little like a Death and Resurrection event, and somehow related to my father's death.

I moved to Los Angeles shortly afterwards, taking Tioutik and Dibidi on the Super Chief train. Dibidi was not spayed and had several litters with neighborhood toughs. Tioutik was killed by a car. Dibidi was a wonderful mother and I couldn't bring myself to give her kittens away. When they were of weaning age, Dibidi grew progressively angrier at me for keeping them around. She and I spoke to each other and understood each other perfectly. There were spooky incidents of total language perception. But where the cats were concerned, she wouldn't forgive me. She wanted me to herself. I got her to relent a bit by taking her to motels for the night where we ate a grilled chicken, just the two of us (I wasn't yet a vegetarian), and then slept in bed together. At the time, it cost my husband and I $5.00 a motel night, which was a big sum, for we were usually broke. It was 1959. But Dibidi understood the sacrifice and the effort, and began to treat me better.

One day in 1960, as I was upstairs in our cantilevered house in the Hollywood Hills, I became suddenly aware of a strange noise. After a while, one of our cats began to inspect the floor. I heard scratching under it, and in a flash I suddenly realized what it was. Dibidi was used to napping down below on the porch near an open window. A dog galloped by and startled her awake. By mistake, instead of jumping into the window, she climbed up a trellis and ended up under the cantilevered floor up above, unable to hold on. She dropped as I bounded down the stairs to catch her. I reached bottom at the same time she did, on some rocks, and broke her spine. She was in shock as we raced her to the vet. She managed to come out of shock and into a body cast. The vet hoped she wouldn't be paralyzed, but she was. I had to move her from side to side every two hours, night and day for weeks. At that time, I was teaching and performing in Instant Theatre. Dibidi lived in a basket, and went with us, my husband and I, everywhere.

When the cast came off, it was clear she wouldn't walk again. She was 6 years old and a paraplegic. The vet said cats couldn't survive being "down". He gave her 6 months to live, maximum. But Dibidi lived another 12 years! She died in my arms, on her own, not assisted, in 1972, aged 18. She went through the process of dying for about an hour, as I had her on my chest, lying on my bed, which was the way she said she wanted it to be. She was purring as her breath grew shorter, and was wearing the "soft furs". She had several coats that she wore for different occasions. She put on the soft furs when she was really happy. When it was time, she looked up at me, stretched her limbs, even the paralyzed ones, said "Maow!" and expired in that position. I stayed crying and petting her for a long time, and she was later buried in our yard, a big sculpture of mine as her tombstone.

Dibidi had lived a perfectly happy life. She had me exactly where she wanted me: as her constant slave! She came with us to New York, to New Jersey, to Big Sur, to San Francisco, to many communities close to Los Angeles where I taught. She came to the Renaissance Faire. She ran and jumped on furniture, and galloped up a creek, me running with her with my hand under her belly, she pulling herself along on her muscular front legs. She learned to go to the bathroom over the toilet as I held her over my knee. She lived through the Laurel Canyon fire, the many electric storms, the Northridge earthquake after we moved to the Valley, a near house fire, and, in my arms always at the first sign of trouble. She never had to worry or be anxious again. At age 18, when she died, she was still the beautiful cat with the strange look in her eyes, and she is forever with me. Her death was ecstatic, and she taught me not to fear dying. She taught me how to live and how to die, with calm, joy, and courage. She showed me how to perform in spite of limitations, and I learned, also suffering from leg trouble myself. To this day, I have named my teaching, my building, and my business after her. Doing by Doing is also her.

A strange coincidence is the fact that, as a little child, I had a recurring dream that always stayed with me: I was on the beach in the South of France, and there, on the sand, was a little girl who was a paraplegic in a wheelchair. I begged my parents to take the little girl home with us, so I could take care of her, and they did. It was a rapturous dream, for some mysterious reason. And strangely enough for an agnostic who doesn't believe in resurrection, or life after death, or transmigration of souls, or reincarnation, I believe in all these things where Dibidi is concerned! I talk to her every day, ask for protection, and when good and amazing things happen, knowing it comes from her, I thank her in gratitude.

So now, you, dear reader, also know what DbD stands for! And it does me good to think that Dibidi will live on in yet another form, in this little book that I dedicate to her.

After the catharsis of the Dibidi story, we all pick up our drums and other instruments, and begin a chant and percussion piece that lasts as long as it wants and needs to. Then we hug and part. That's the end of The DbD Experience weekend, but not the end of the experience, as letters from alumni can attest.

Dibidi collage by Rachel Rosenthal (detail)

Addenda: Post-DbD Letters

Choosing these letters was extremely difficult. There are so many, and each is distinct and addresses a different aspect of the experience. Here are just a few of those wonderful glimpses into people's individual reactions. Thanks to all of you, and to all those whose letters I haven't included.

> *Rachel,*
>
> *I am sitting down to write you at more length because of my joy and gratitude about dbd and the dbd weekend. It really was a soul-scraping and soul-cleansing experience. It made me understand, deeply and in a new way, the power of the moment and of chance. ("Chance knows what it is doing" is unforgettable.) These things I knew intellectually—who doesn't admire John Cage? etc., but I had never really tried them out, much less lived them along my pulse, as I was FORCED to (gracias a dios) at dbd. Friday and Saturday were agony for me! I felt clumsy and stupid, as my ego was scraped raw and white like an onion. I watched the lithe beautiful boys and girls do everything beautifully, I stumbled into the costume room to snatch minimal bits of costume, breathless and sure that I would make the wrong choices. I did what I could do on stage, mostly without my favorite tool for stage-dominance, language. No fake Shakespeare, no funny accents, and no TIME to prepare anything.*
>
> *Meanwhile, I felt that you were quite severe with us—holding us to very high standards, exactly as if we had had months to prepare and rehearse.*
>
> *Of course I knew very well what was happening—I really did—your intensity with us, the very pointed critique, was uniting with the lack of preparation time to create a higher and higher quality of spontaneity. I felt that I was simultaneously surrendering more fully to the moment AND in that surrender I was making better and better decisions based on a desire to NOT DISAPPOINT RACHEL!*

My ego deflation reached a critical, and spiritual, point on Sunday, at which I no longer worried. The solo/duo piece—Love—was a huge turning point. I honestly had no idea what I was going to do, other than pull something red out of myself, as late as thirty seconds before Shana and I went on. I decided to invest in disaster. I would simply go ahead. I was past caring what I looked like onstage. All I knew was that I would do something physical—to show you that I could—and that I would pull that red thing—a schmatta?—from my breast.

Then everything lined up miraculously. I found the red string to yank out of my heart, at about fifteen seconds and counting. I could use the vertical climbing cloth to pull myself up with. Wonderful generous dbders asked me how they could help me with my part of the set. Somebody snaked a black schmatta across half the stage. Okay, I could snake around in that. My vague idea was a kind of struggle with divine love. Eyes out!

I writhed and said some words about struggle. I could see that Shana was preparing a Banquet of Divine Love, horizontally, to complement my (eventual) verticality. Ariadna was her usual genius self on the violin. I wanted to marry them both.

The critique was wonderful. In talking about my "script" you invoked Beckett, who is a real touchstone of mine because of the transformation he went through (he narrates it in Krapp's Last Tape) between a too-smart imitator of Joyce (his terrible book Dream of Fair to Middling Women shows him in that mode) and the Beckett we know—and it came when he embraced his melancholy, his depression. I have always thought that this was the most instructive and moving creative metamorphosis in all of artistic history, short of Walt Whitman's mysterious transformation from a mediocre newspaperman and party hack into Walt Whitman, but we have no idea how that happened. I learned good points about my blocking and my voice. But the thing had come together pretty damn well between the yin of dbd (trust the moment) and the yang (internalize Rachel's theatrical values! And quickly!)

In retrospect I realized that you had maintained this perfect Taoistical balance of yang and yin throughout: high standards, the good old kind—you are of my father's generation and I heard his values heightened in you, like respect for the audience, intolerance of the mere idea for its own sake, clarity, the value of esthetic distance between audience and performer, and many more—plus . . . "Instant Theater:" the whole heritage of the most radical kind of instantaneity, from Cage, from the Abstract Expressionists, from Dada and Fluxus and mainly from your own experience. The combination was life-changing for me, because I had always brought these two values together in my work, but they were AT WAR! My sense of Standards killed my spontaneity, and the result was worry. Dbd forced the two *values into a fusion over the three days. Everything and everyone contributed to this fusion, which was warm and colorful. You always blended this warm soup of creative openness with a sharp critical sense, so that finally it was impossible to tell where the one value left off and the other began.*

So, as I said in an earlier note, I am now working on my one-person piece, which is not very abstract or theater-poetical, but for which dbd works brilliantly And thanks to you also I am finding ways to make the overall movement and rhythm of the piece much deeper as I am holding myself open to the poetry that the piece possesses and am discovering more and more of it. So what began as a sort of Robin Williams multi-character comedy schtick will probably end up somewhere in Robert Wilson land . . . and I have never seen that before, so it could be fun.

I devoutly wish I were in the eight-week sequence, and hope I have a chance to do it soon. There's a little hideaway I can borrow from Minneapolis movie-industry friends up in the hills about six blocks from Grauman's Chinese, and I'll rent a Chevy Aveo, and get tacos at Cinco De Mayo on Sepulveda and Washington Place, and come and see you and the dogs and everybody, and work, and be in heaven.

Love,

Jon

Note: I've included this letter verbatim because it seems to express so beautifully how one person experienced DbD. RR

Dear Rachel,

I took the workshop so many years ago, but many of the moments still play in my head. The most memorable was the climb to the pinnacle and the meditation that occurred at the top.

I was amazed at how I felt as I climbed that sheer wall. Most people looking at me would have thought that I was groveling on the floor, But it sure took a lot of energy to reach the top of the cliff.

I can't remember what our instructions were when we reached the pinnacle. I think it was basically to react to that moment of accomplishment and location. What it ended up being started as sighs of relief at reaching the top, then an exultation at the tremendous landscape that we viewed. The exultations took form of what I call Toning. Long sustained vowels.

At first we were in the "official" exercise, then we started being thrilled by the sound and the sensation of the vibrations in the undulating chord clusters. We danced with the undulations and sang, and danced and sang. Rachel never stops an exercise. We stop when we are finished. The nature of the sound was infinite. I started wondering how we were going to stop, or if I should stop singing. But I didn't want to, the flow was so intoxicating. We went on for quite awhile. My practical self would pop in every once in a while to wonder if it was "time" now.

The answer would always be, "later".

Then there came a moment that the voices formed a perfectly in tune major chord. It sounded so profound in relationship to the clusters that we had been singing that it took my breath away. It must have done the same to all who were singing, because we all stopped singing at the exact same moment. No choir director could have wished for a better cut off.

We all felt the wonderment. I will never forget that moment.

I am a professional singer and composer. There is no way to say what I learned about music that day.

Health and gladness to you

Judith

Dear Rachel,

How does one begin a post-DbD letter? My life is forever changed by the events that transpired in your studio. I grew as an artist and person during the workshop. As we sank into the core of the earth, journeyed to the stars, grew roots like plants, morphed into amoebas, octopi and other strange creatures, it seemed as if threads of energy unfurled like tendrils from each person in our group and reached beyond the white walls of your studio into the world outside to create ripples of creative energy reverberating outward. You led us to create visual maps of the ways in which we are interconnected to all things simply with our bodies and props.

The "Object Exercise" was difficult for me, but I think that it is really important. I am an animist to a certain extent and think that objects can carry energy and have a life of their own. The object(s) you gave me threw me for a loop. Even so, after a few moments of staring at that metal vase (I'm not even sure that's what it was) and the purple glove, memories of my childhood started to surface. I thought about how I never believed in Santa Claus or ghosts when I was a kid. I went back to a part of my life where I had disbelief in all things fantastic (which I think is ironically linked to my religious upbringing) through an object I'd had no previous relationship with, which is fantastic in its own right. The only thing that wasn't fantastic, probably, was watching it, ha ha.

The "Hidden Aspect" absolutely terrified me. I dreaded going on stage to share that particularly angry shadow of mine . . . but I did it. I'm curious as to the history of that exercise, where you learned it, if you made it up and why? The type of performance that burns into my memory the most is that which presents a character who shares their vulnerabilities while standing in Power in front of an audience. Now I have another way of getting that deep with my own work . . . what baggage do I have that I would prefer others to not know about? Why don't I want them to know about it? Can I transform that into a performance that creates reflection and dialogue about important issues?

You speak so beautifully. It seemed as if words floated from your mouth directly to my heart all weekend. I am so glad to have been able to learn from you, hear your stories, watch you move and make weird noises, and to meet your dogs (although I never really hung out with Mrs. Moore much, just watched her exhibitionism). I will never forget when you roared like a lion at Julia until Sasha intervened, told someone who was having trouble with a voice exercise to just say, "FUCK IT!" over and over again, when you played the drum and sang after telling us about DbD the legendary cat, challenged us to create a bakery scene overrun by poets, to be mice, to be in love, and many, many more moments. Also, I have never worn so many different dresses in a weekend. Really.

I want to come back and take more workshops with you. A weekend just seems too short. One can never blow it out their ass or experiment with different ways in which to embody the words "humiliation" or "juiciness" too many times in a lifetime.

I hope to work with you again,

Rae

Dear Rachel,

Thank you so much for the DbD Experience. I got a great deal from the sessions. Steeped in psychological realism, I was excited to be introduced to other choices. The parallels you draw from the visual arts—cubism, abstract expressionism, surrealism, et al, really inspired and expanded me. I was also helped by your emphasis on collaboration, and heartened by your specific guidance on the elements that go into a piece. Your emphasis on being clear and specific was just what I needed. But most important for me was the realization that I must trust the process more, trust my talent, my collaborators, my audience . . .

Joanie

Dear Rachel,

I have thought often of the Doing by Doing workshop you taught here in Ottawa. You served as a catalyst in my life, precipitating a major change. I want to express my deep gratitude to you for showing me the way to what feels like my true destiny. In case you have forgotten me, I worked as an administrator at the gallery. I had been a visual artist and felt I had lost my voice, or vision or whatever. You showed me the way to another creative outlet that, I see now, is one for which I am far better suited . . . As part of my warm-up exercise before performing, I still do the 10 minute head roll you taught us, and invariably, I see you in my minds-eye and remember all the wonderful places you guided us to in the workshop—from the fiery breathing bowels of the earth, to the infinite expanse of the cosmos. Thank you for continuing inspiration.

Paulette

Dear Rachel,

Greetings from the East Coast. The DbD was an incredible experience for me and I wanted to write and share with you what I got out of that time in your presence. The first and most important feeling I have noticed since the DbD is I have my body back. I am not afraid of touching or being touched. I have spent many years separated from my body. It is the cosmic joke of being a dancer—I find so many of my peers suffer the same sense of separation from their bodies. Maybe that's why we dance. Otherwise we would simply float away into our heads. Now I am in my body and experiencing life in an entirely new way. This is a powerful change for me. I am no longer interested in investigating the WHY of my feelings, or the WHEN DID I START FEELING THIS WAY. I spent a long time doing that! I am interested in changing what is blocking my experience of being fully human and moving on. That happened in the short time we were together. This has greatly improved my relationship with my husband-to-be and my relationship with my own work. As I grow into my mature adulthood I am looking for positive models of growing older as a performing artist. There are not many, but I feel I have found one in you. Being with you and seeing how you shared what you learned from your life experience was a powerful teaching in itself . . . you taught with a clear, direct and loving heart. I hope to be a teacher like you someday . . . BJ

Here are some excerpts of letters from participants in the DbD Workshop for People Living With HIV/AIDS, held in September 1993.

Dear Wonderful Rachel,

What can I say about last weekend's DbD Experience for People with HIV/AIDS? What I cannot say is that it transformed my life because prior to the weekend I didn't have a life anymore so how could it be transformed?? What I can say is that the weekend gave me back my life in a powerful and conscious way; once again I am living—albeit with AIDS—instead of just waiting to die of it.

. . . I'm once again alive with the possibilities of passion and transformation. Thank you seems too simple, but from the essence of my being I thank you and honor you.

Wayne

Dear Rachel,

This letter is being written with much gratitude. What you have created was one of, if not the most healing experiences of my life. As you witnessed, my strength increased tenfold. What a great gift you offer. Your techniques are truly unique and remarkable. I learned from every person who was involved. I hope this great DbD Experience is shared with as many human beings as possible. Keep these DbD's going, please! So many people need to reconnect to what we pretend isn't there—so we can survive and really live.

Love,

Dennis

Los Angeles, January 1st, 2009.

My first DbD was in February 2004. I had four DbD experiences, the last one being as a "Slave of Love".

Each workshop has been a major step in my development as an artist and along the years, I have found in Rachel Rosenthal the teacher that you trust and never leave; my sensei. And I will keep learning from her as long as I live.

I remember with sweetness the feeling I had during Rachel Rosenthal's first talk for the DbD opening. I immediately felt that, for the first time in my life, I was aware and conscious; to be at the right place at the right moment in the universe. And when Rachel Rosenthal said "be content with your place in the Universe", there I was, in perfect connection with that perfect moment. It felt that what I always wanted to be was finally going to emerge, and, it did.

For the first time, my artist soul was valued, honored and nourished, prized and treasured, respected, encouraged, and understood. Everything was making sense, and my vision was lucid. I left the DbD experience with knowledge. I learnt some fundamentals on which my career as an artist would spring. I learnt, and then I knew: I knew what was my mission on earth, I knew why I was an artist, I knew why it was difficult, I knew why I couldn't do anything else but it, I knew how great it was. And I wanted to celebrate. An immense sense of joy and excitement filled my body, my desire to make art was connected to my inspiration, everything felt like bound and free flow at the same time, everything felt real, true, alive, and oh . . . how exciting. "Remain true to yourself, feel joy, give thanks, feel gratitude", she said. I was ready to struggle for my path, my choices, my call, my mission.

DbD brought me to be in touch with myself, my artist soul, my vocation, my why-am-I-on-this-earth, why do I feel so much, why do I desire so much to make this happen, why do I want so much to do this as my profession, why am I so different. Desires for fame and success were not important. My inner deepest drive for my art was what mattered.

I had been carried by my passion through difficult experiences that were in my way for becoming an artist, and I would fight sometimes against my own determinism. I was wondering why I would choose a complicated path, while a common path was possible to take. But always, I had to keep going, "I couldn't not be an artist" and I had to "remain true to myself". After the DbD experience, I finally gave gratitude to my struggles, and I was able to honor and contemplate them. I became my best friend. And I decided to honor my mission and role. There was so much to do, I had so much work, how exciting.

Rachel Rosenthal said "if you are a hero, you answer the call". Working with her was a call, and being part of her company, I am a hero.

Nathalie

Postscript, June 2009

After the DbD Experience, students are encouraged to do the eight-week class, eight weekly sessions of four hours each, culminating in a public weekend of performances culled from workshop assignments. This workshop deepens the areas of theatrical creativity opened in the DbD, and takes the participants further into skill and imagination. I will follow this book with another covering the eight-week class.